AUTHENTIC VICTORIAN DECORATION AND ORNAMENTATION

in Full Color

46 Plates from "Studies in Design"

by

CHRISTOPHER DRESSER

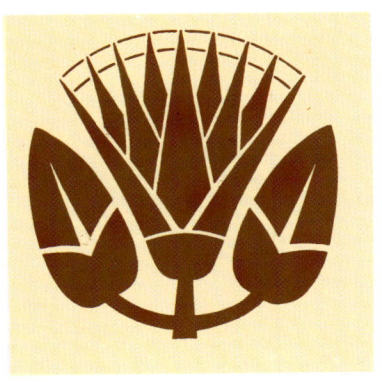

Dover Publications, Inc., New York

PUBLISHER'S NOTE

Victorian England was blessed with a seemingly inexhaustible supply of individuals of great ability, ambition and energy. Among their number was Christopher Dresser (1834–1904), a pioneer in the field of industrial design, botanist, teacher, traveler and entrepreneur. He received his training at the Government School of Design in London from 1847 to 1854; his first published work was a plate in Owen Jones's *The Grammar of Ornament* (1856), one of the most influential stylebooks of the period. The style Dresser evolved—virile, almost spiky—was softened after a visit to Japan in 1876. Gradually easing his rather strict adherence to geometrics, he developed a style that put him in favor during the flowering of Art Nouveau. The pottery, silver and glassware he designed often struck a balance between utility and decoration that years later would be echoed in the Bauhaus.

The present work consists of a selection of 46 of the 60 plates that, along with a 40-page text, comprised *Studies in Design*, published by Cassell, Petter and Galpin, London, in monthly installments between 1874 and 1876. The plates, most of them chromolithographs, dramatically demonstrate the culmination of Dresser's earlier style. Most of the designs are based on plants and florals, reflecting Dresser's background in botany (in 1860 Jena University had conferred the degree of Doctor of Philosophy upon him for work in that field). But in his designs, the plant forms have undergone rigorous treatment: He has, for the most part, stylized and subjected them to a rigid geometrical construction and arrangement, so much so that page 22 looks like pure Art Deco. Such designs were anathema to the advocates of the Arts and Crafts movement, who, while aspiring to elevate the tastes of all, actually produced works so expensive that they were only within the means of the wealthy. Dresser designed with the intention of making his works available, if not to everyone, then certainly to a wider market. The antithesis of William Morris, he embraced new technology.

The motifs in *Studies in Design* were intended to be applied to ceilings, dadoes, borders, corners, panels, etc. The captions, expressing these purposes, are modified from Dresser's. Styles represented include adaptations from the Gothic, Chinese and Islamic, among others, as well as inventions that are Dresser's alone. Calling him "perhaps the greatest of commercial designers," an anonymous appreciation of Dresser that appeared in *The Studio* (November 1899, pp. 104–114) said specifically of these plates: ". . . they may be justly credited with vigour, originality, and perfect regard for the materials for which they were designed; . . . we can but approve their ingenuity, the fertile invention they display, and their wise respect for precedent which seeks to revere the spirit of past styles while discarding the letter."

Copyright © 1986 by Dover Publications, Inc.
All rights reserved under Pan American and International Copyright Conventions.

Published in Canada by General Publishing Company, Ltd., 30 Lesmill Road, Don Mills, Toronto, Ontario.
Published in the United Kingdom by Constable and Company, Ltd.

This Dover edition, first published in 1986, is a new selection of plates from *Studies in Design*, originally published by Cassell, Petter and Galpin, London, 1874–76. The Publisher's Note and captions, based on the original text, were specially prepared for the present edition.

DOVER *Pictorial Archive* SERIES

Authentic Victorian Decoration and Ornamentation in Full Color: 46 Plates from "Studies in Design" belongs to the Dover Pictorial Archive Series. Up to four illustrations may be reproduced on any one project or in any single publication, free and without special permission. Wherever possible, include a credit line indicating the title of this book, author and publisher. Please address the publisher for permission to make more extensive use of illustrations in this book than that authorized above.
The reproduction of this book in whole is prohibited.

Manufactured in the United States of America
Dover Publications, Inc., 31 East 2nd Street, Mineola, N.Y. 11501

Library of Congress Cataloging in Publication Data

Dresser, Christopher.
  Authentic Victorian decoration and ornamentation in full color.

  (Dover pictorial archive series)
  1. Decoration and ornament, Victorian—Themes, motives. 2. Decoration and ornament—Plant forms.
  I. Dresser, Christopher. Studies in design. II. Title. III. Series.
NK1565.D73   1986   745.4'4924   85-29305
ISBN 0-486-25083-0

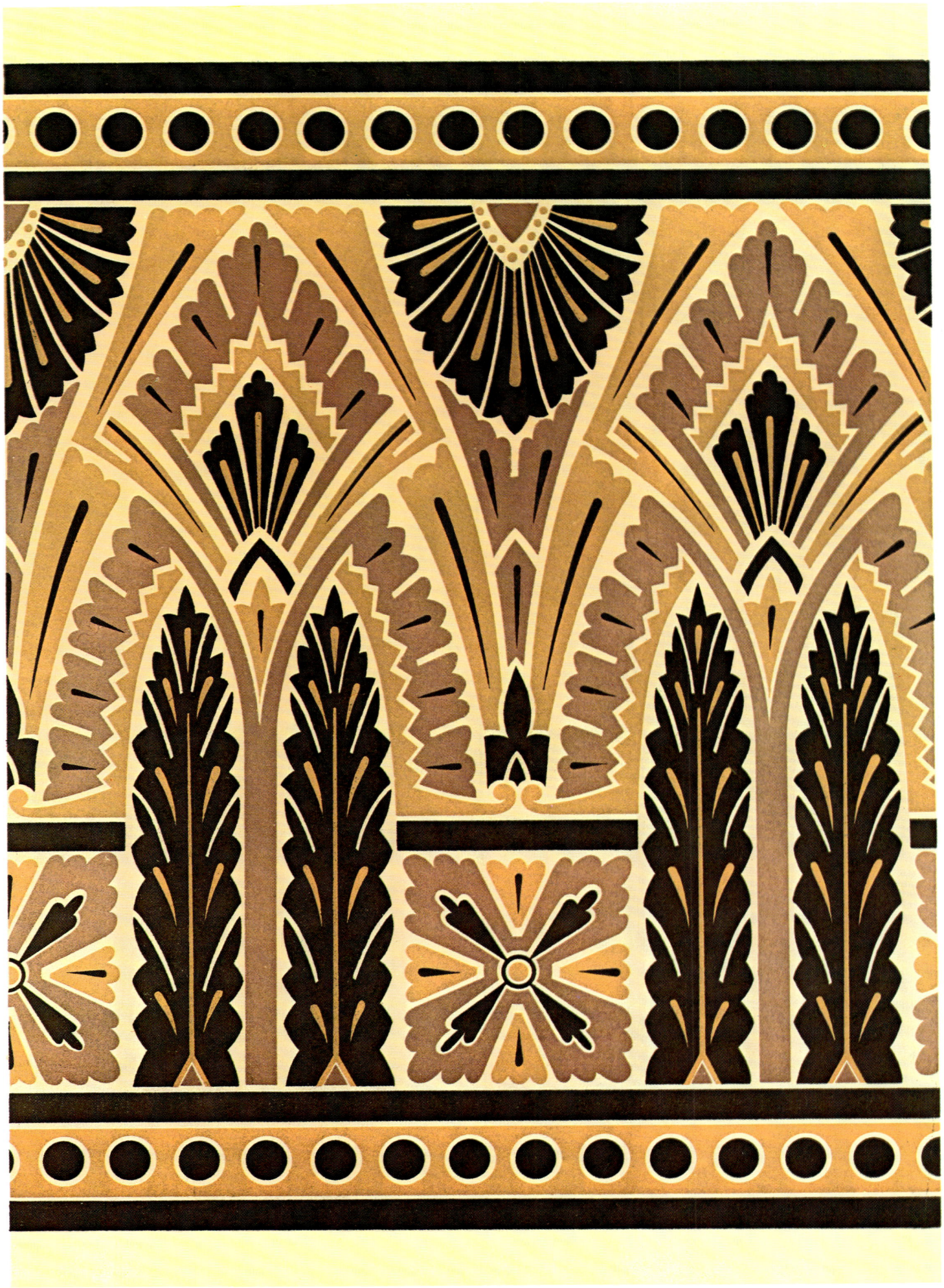

Frieze for a wall.

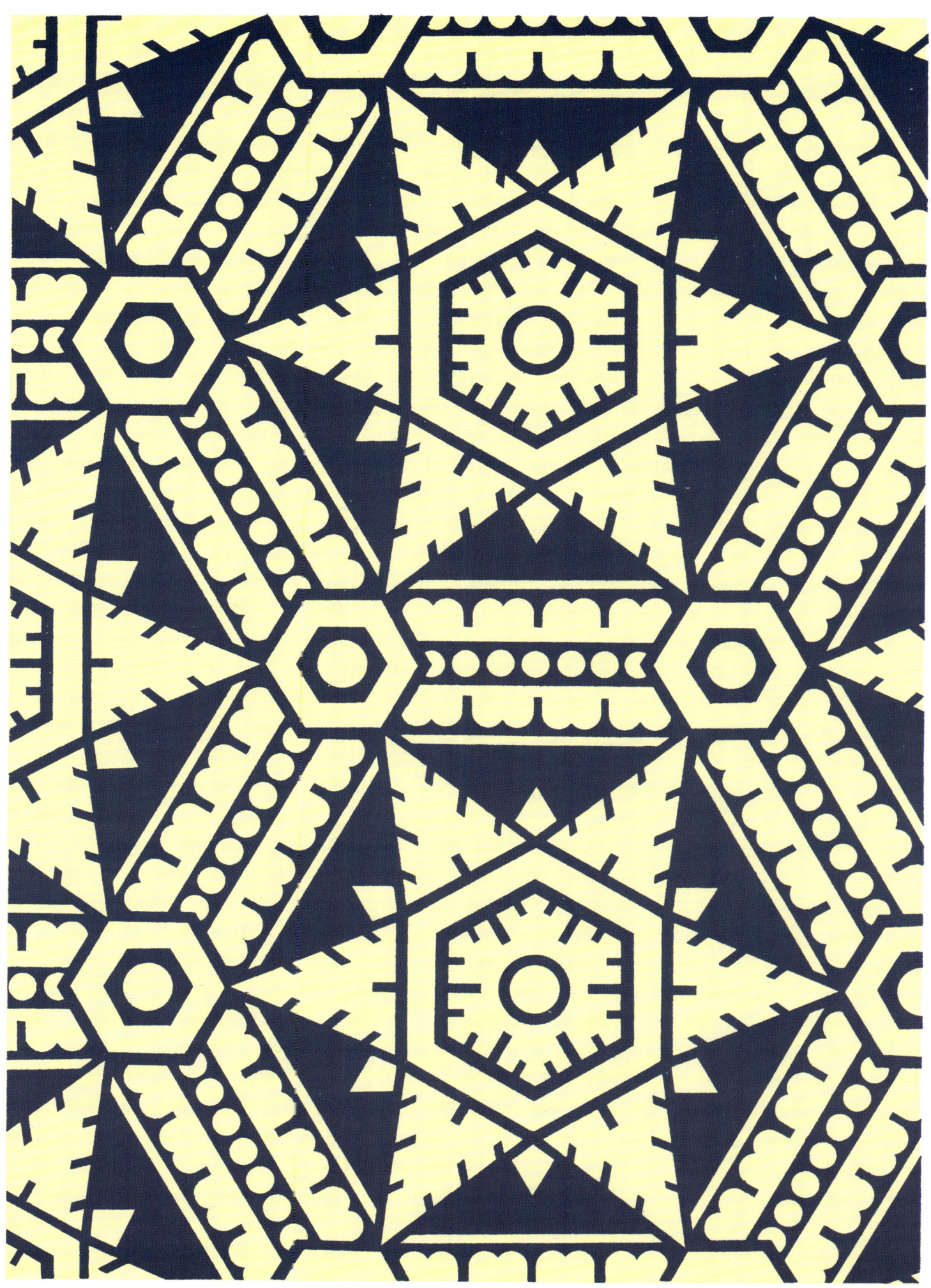

Ceiling pattern.

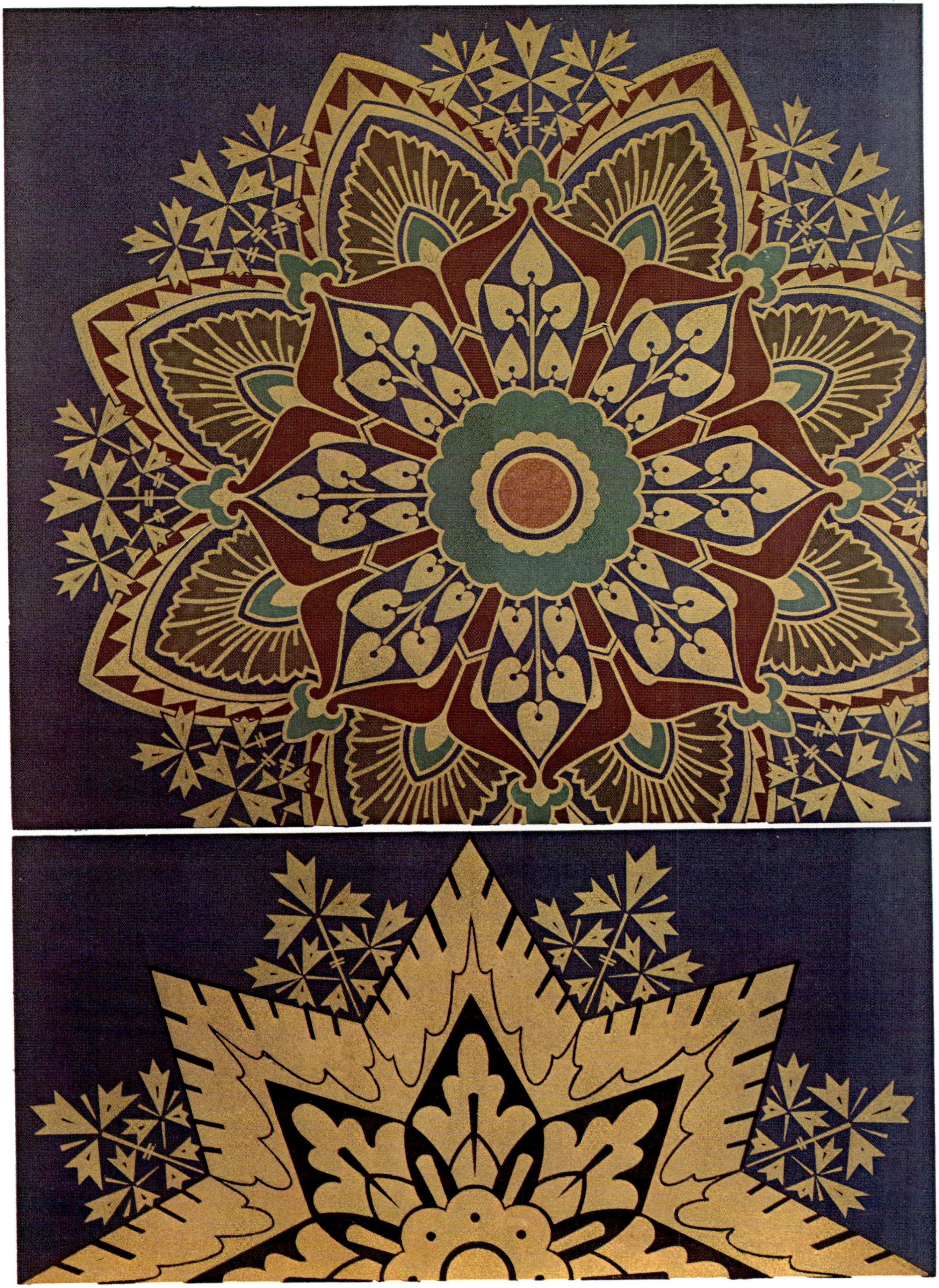

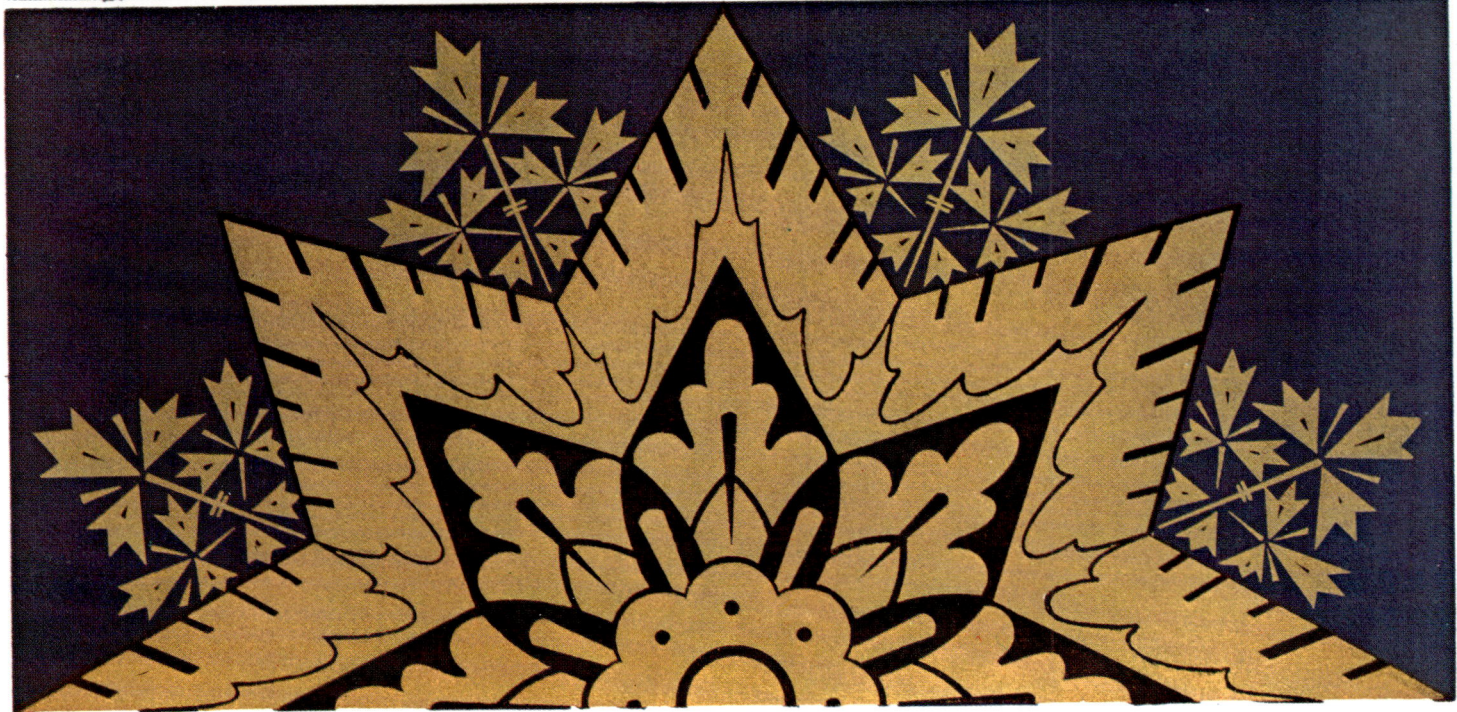

Two decorations for ceilings.

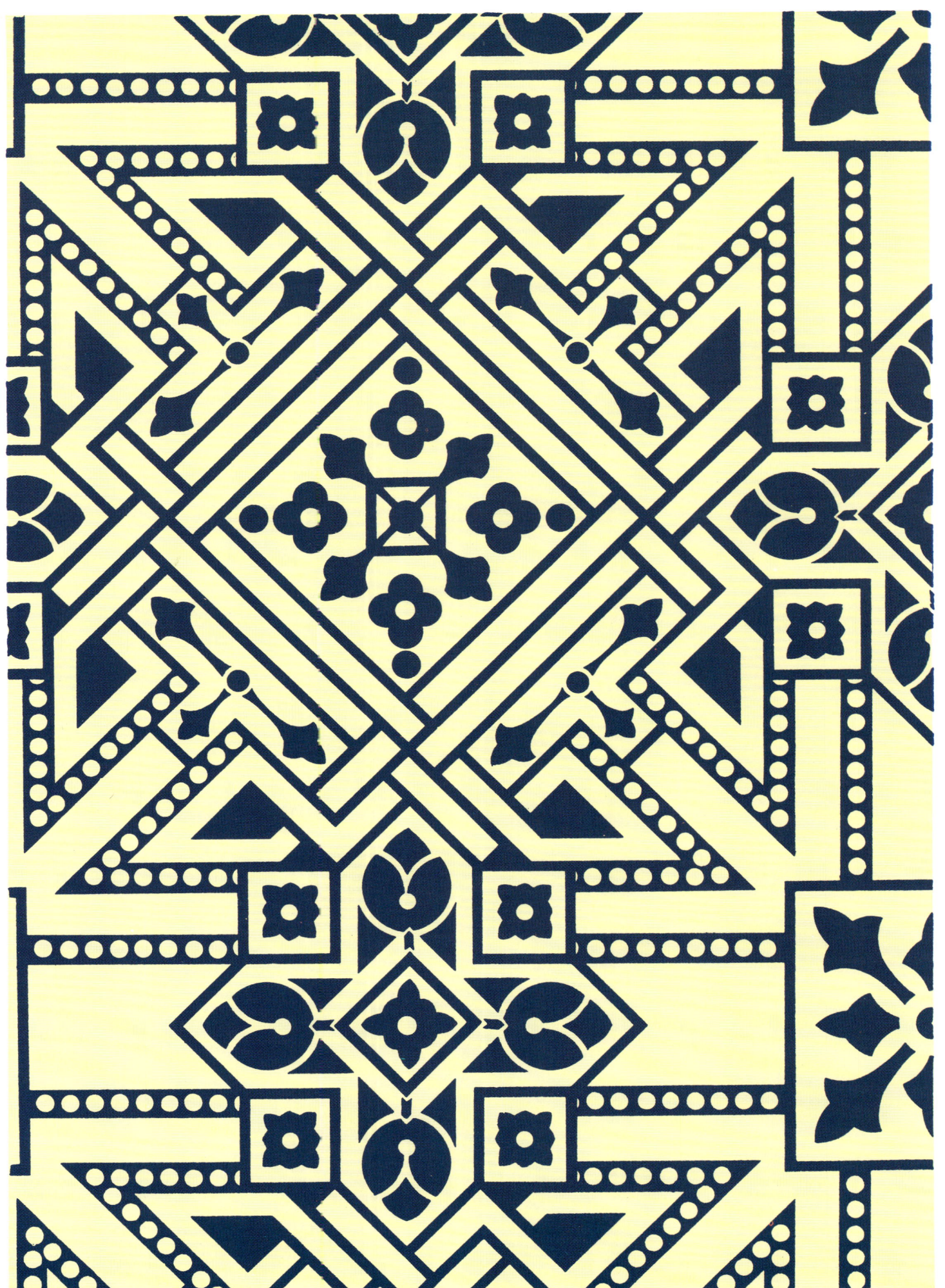

Ceiling pattern.

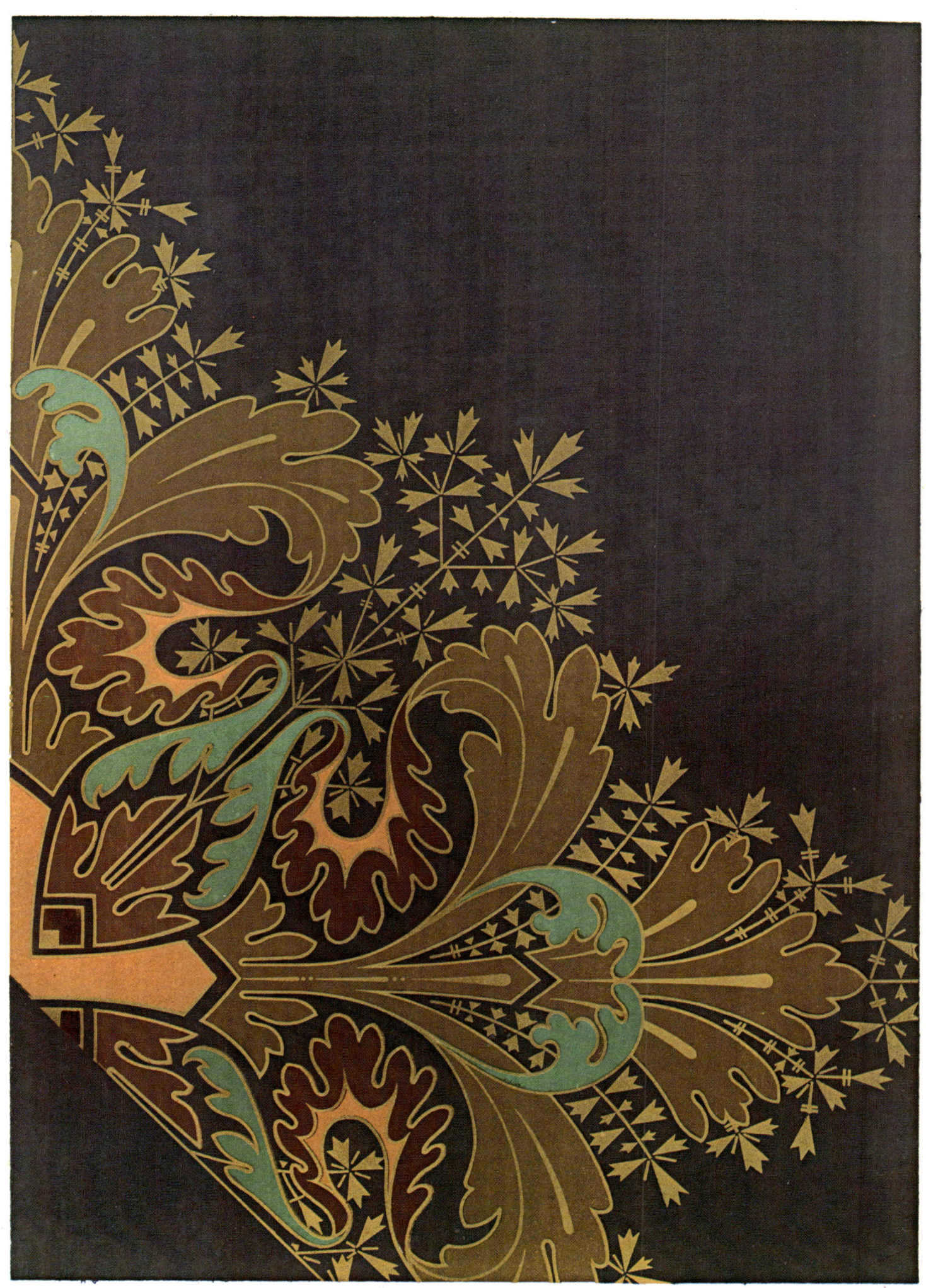
Ornament for the center of a ceiling.

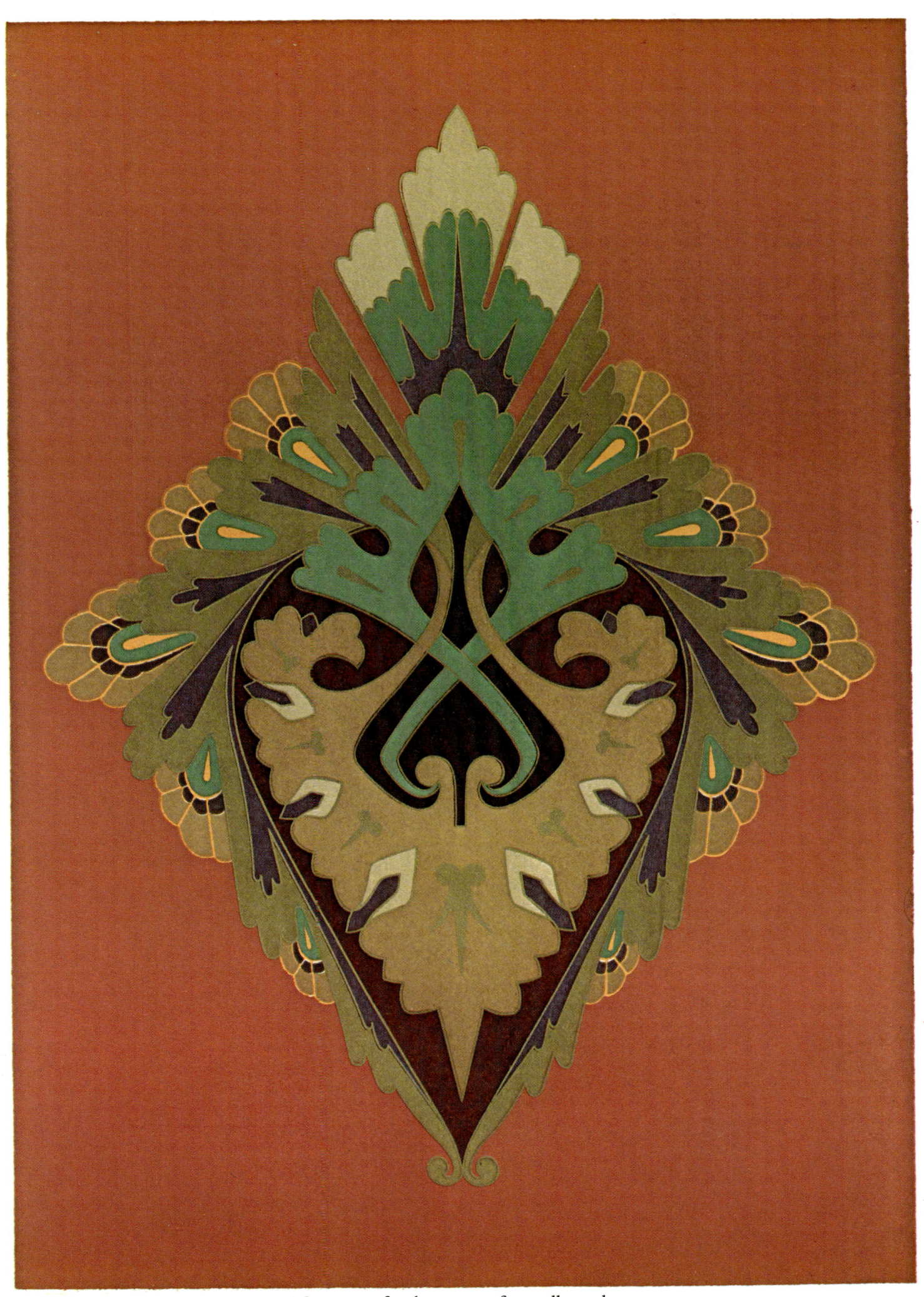
Ornament for the center of a small panel.

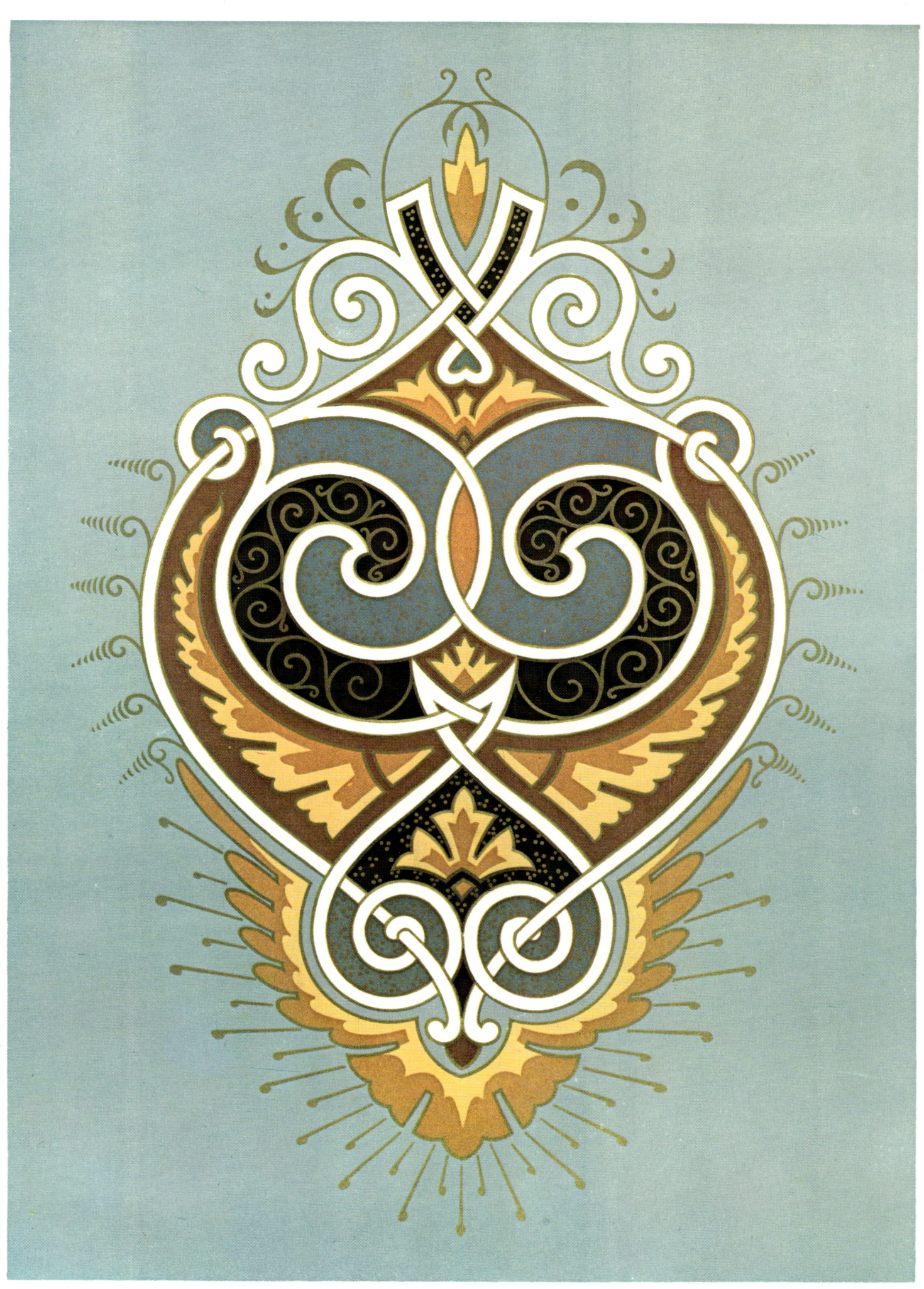

Ornament for the center of a panel.

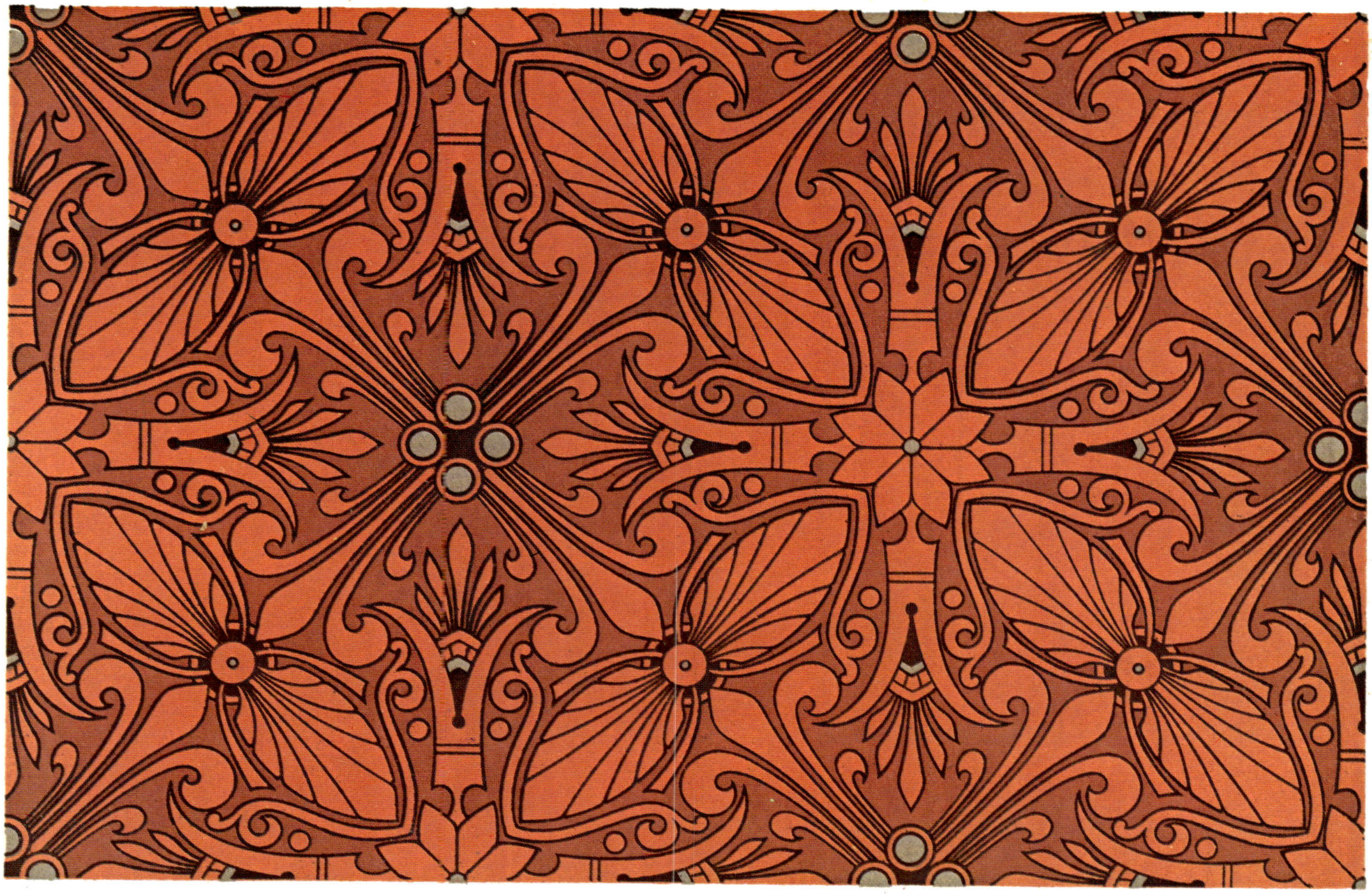

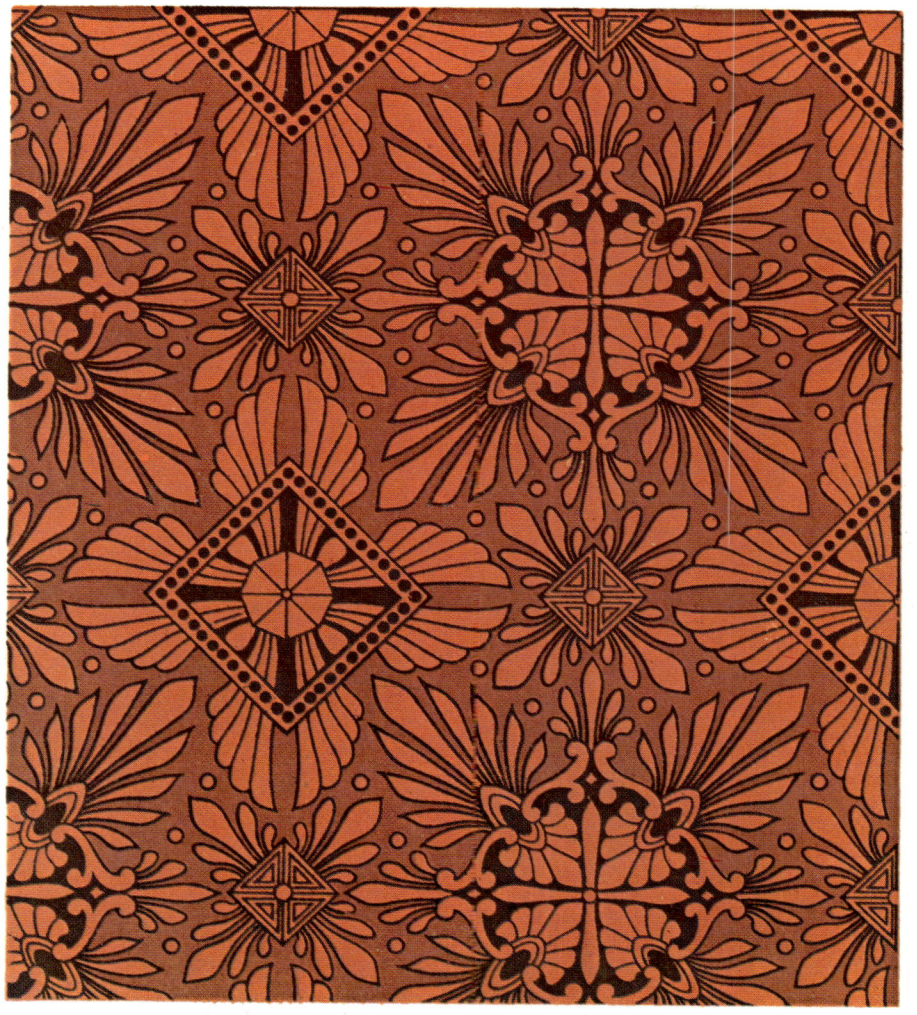
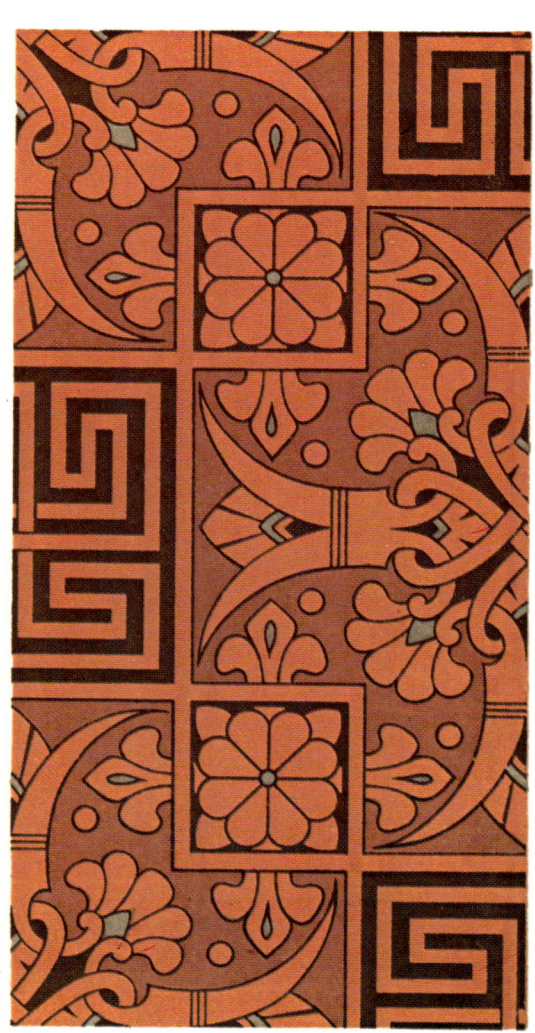

Dado ornaments.

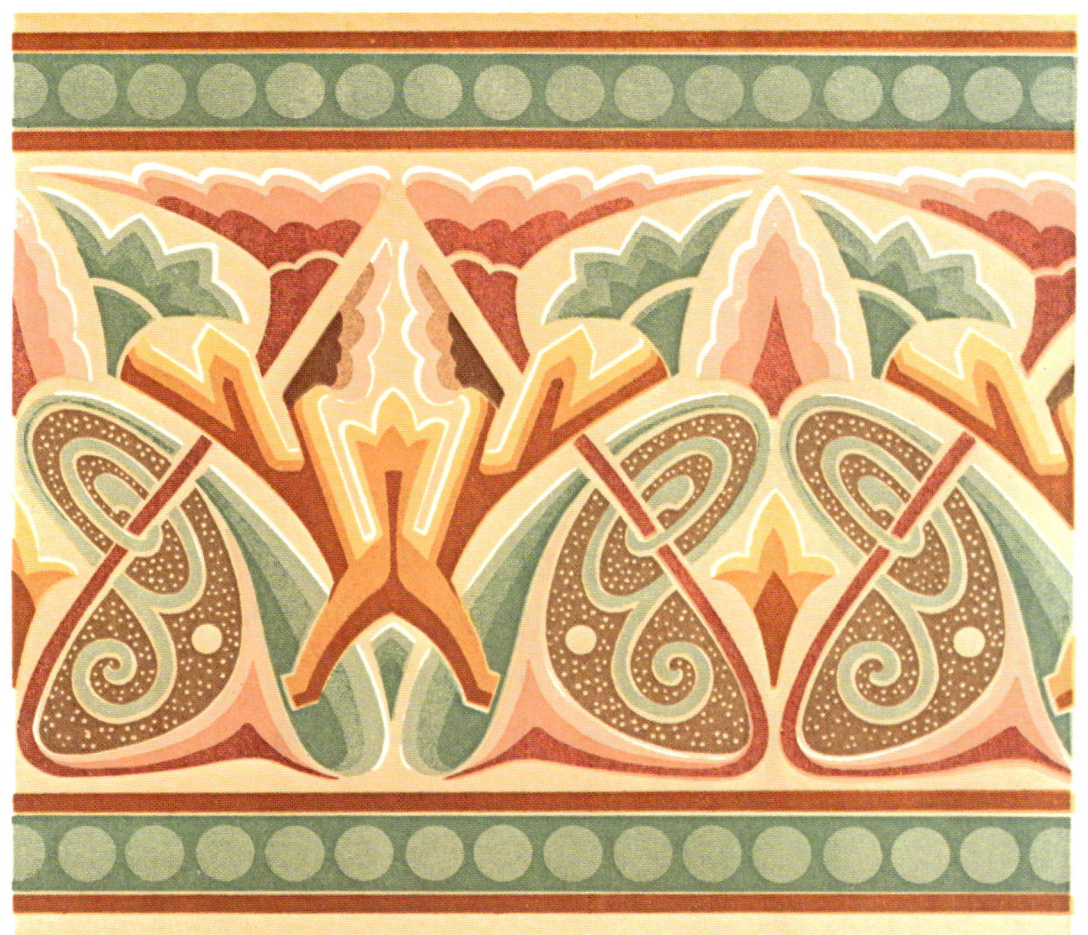

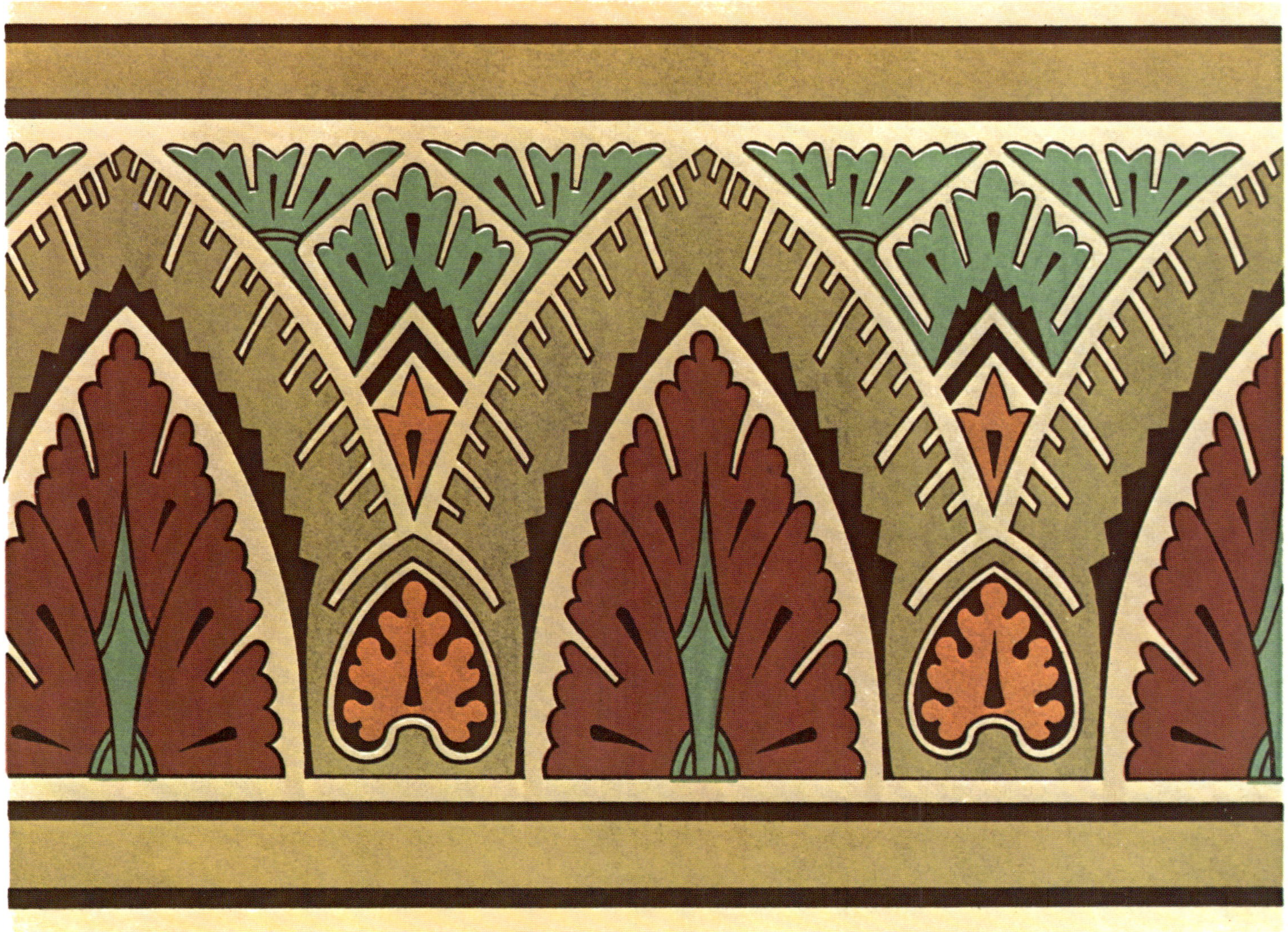

Two frieze or dado-rail ornaments.

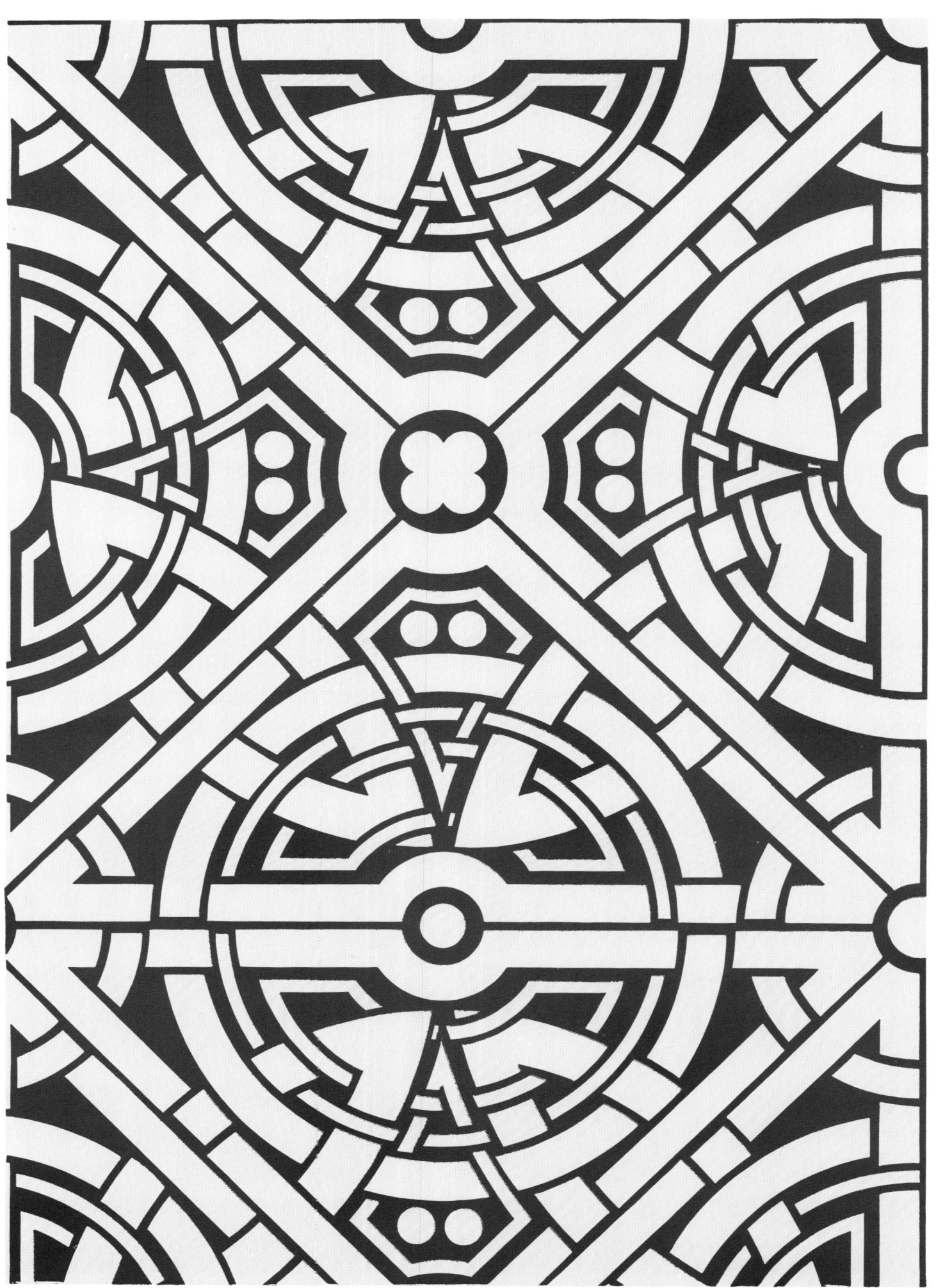

Ceiling decoration.

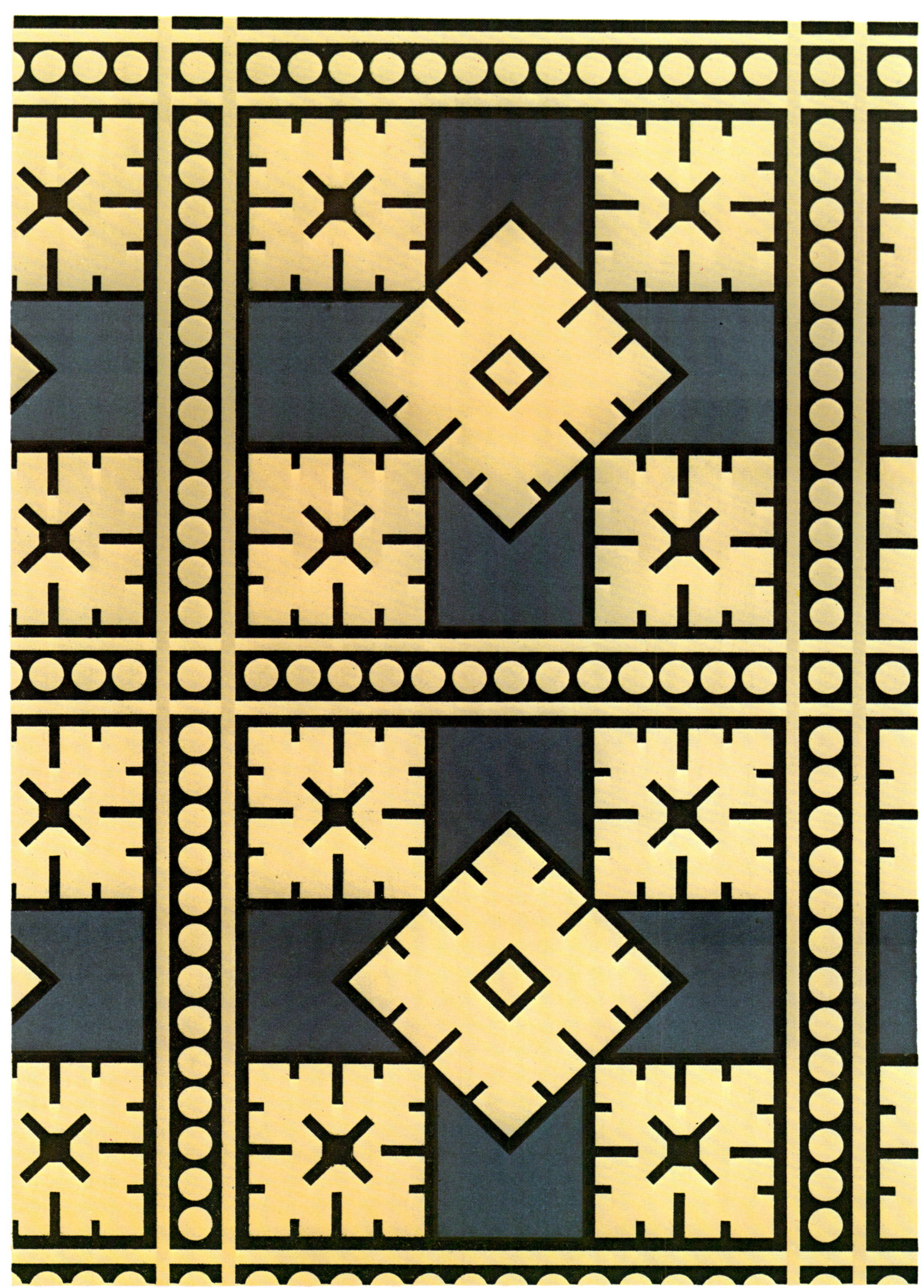
Allover ornament for a ceiling.

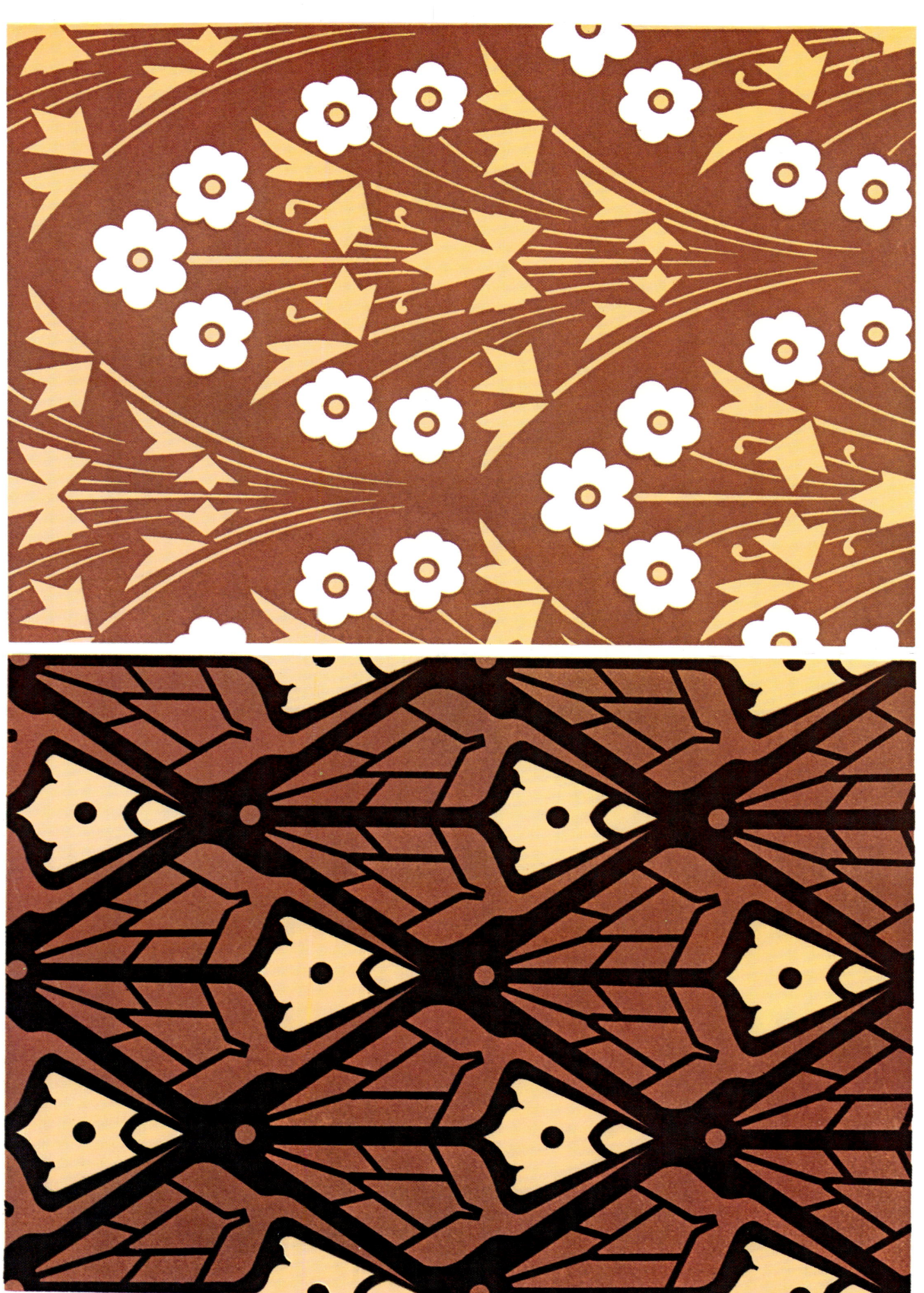

Two wall patterns.

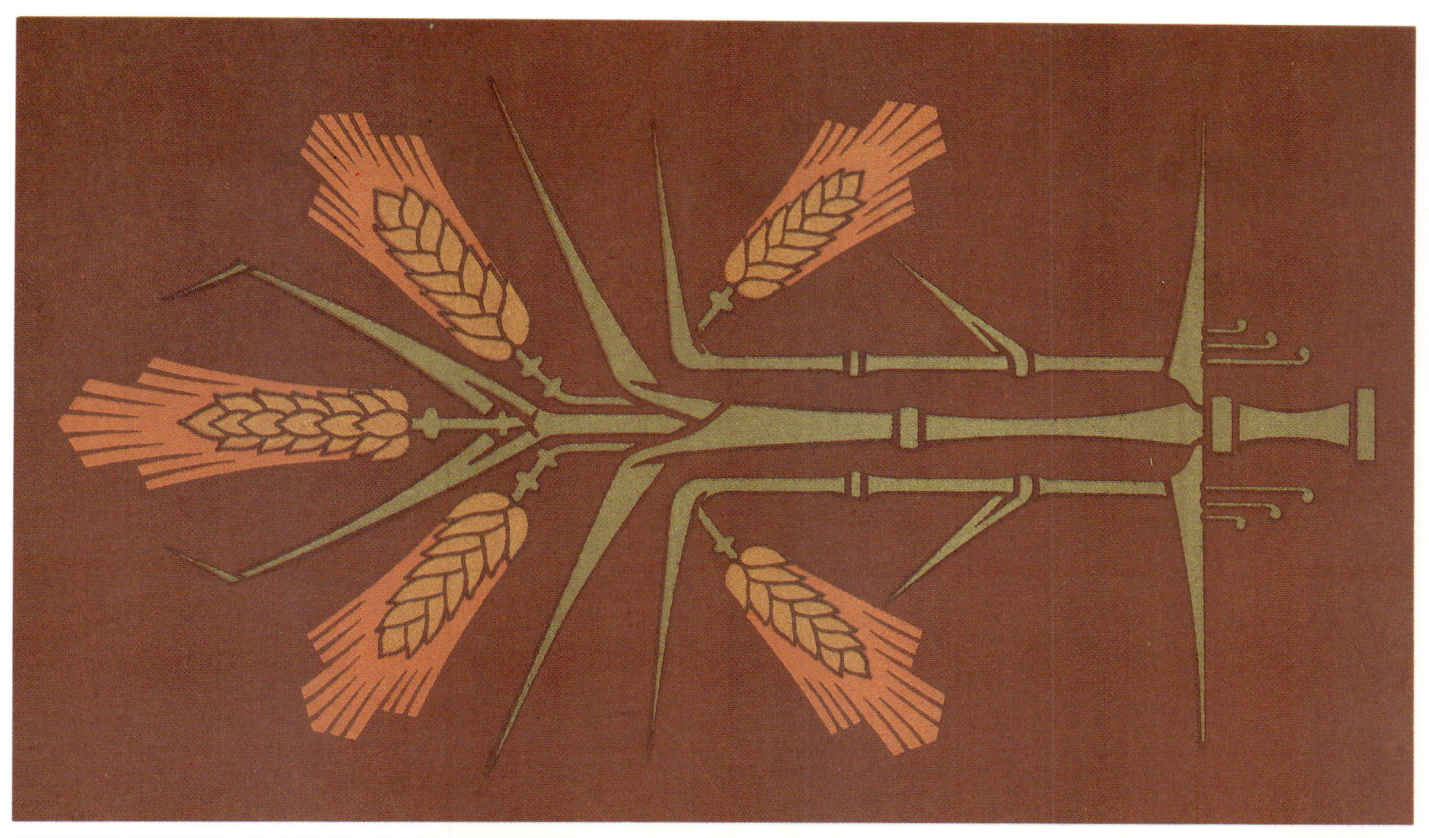
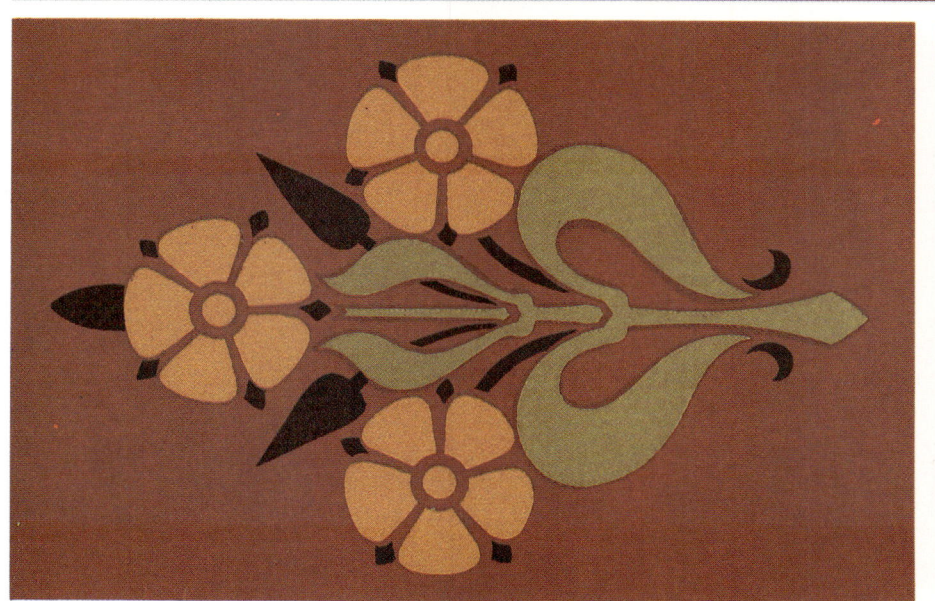

Powderings for walls or dadoes.

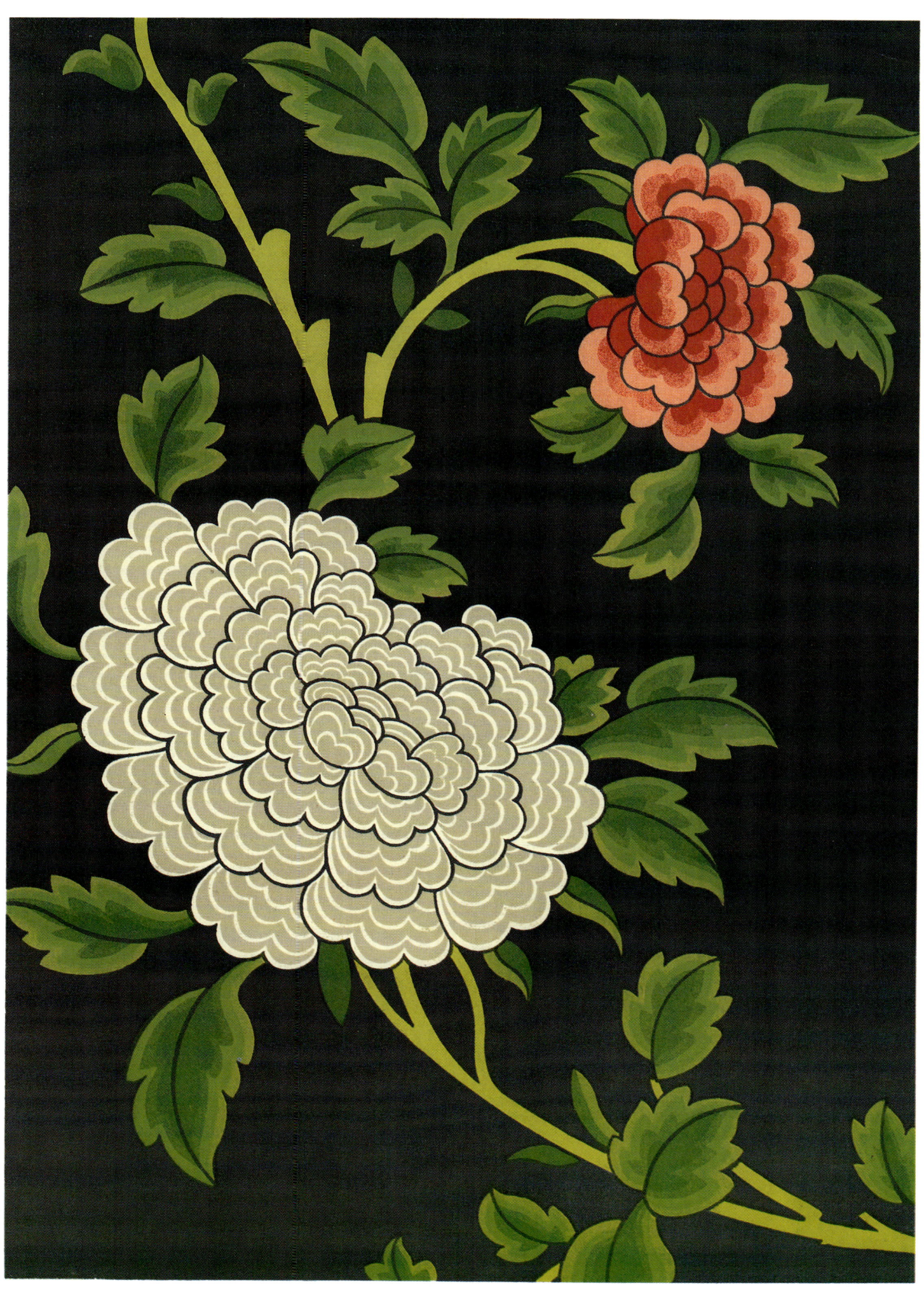

Adaptation of a Chinese ornament for a wall decoration.

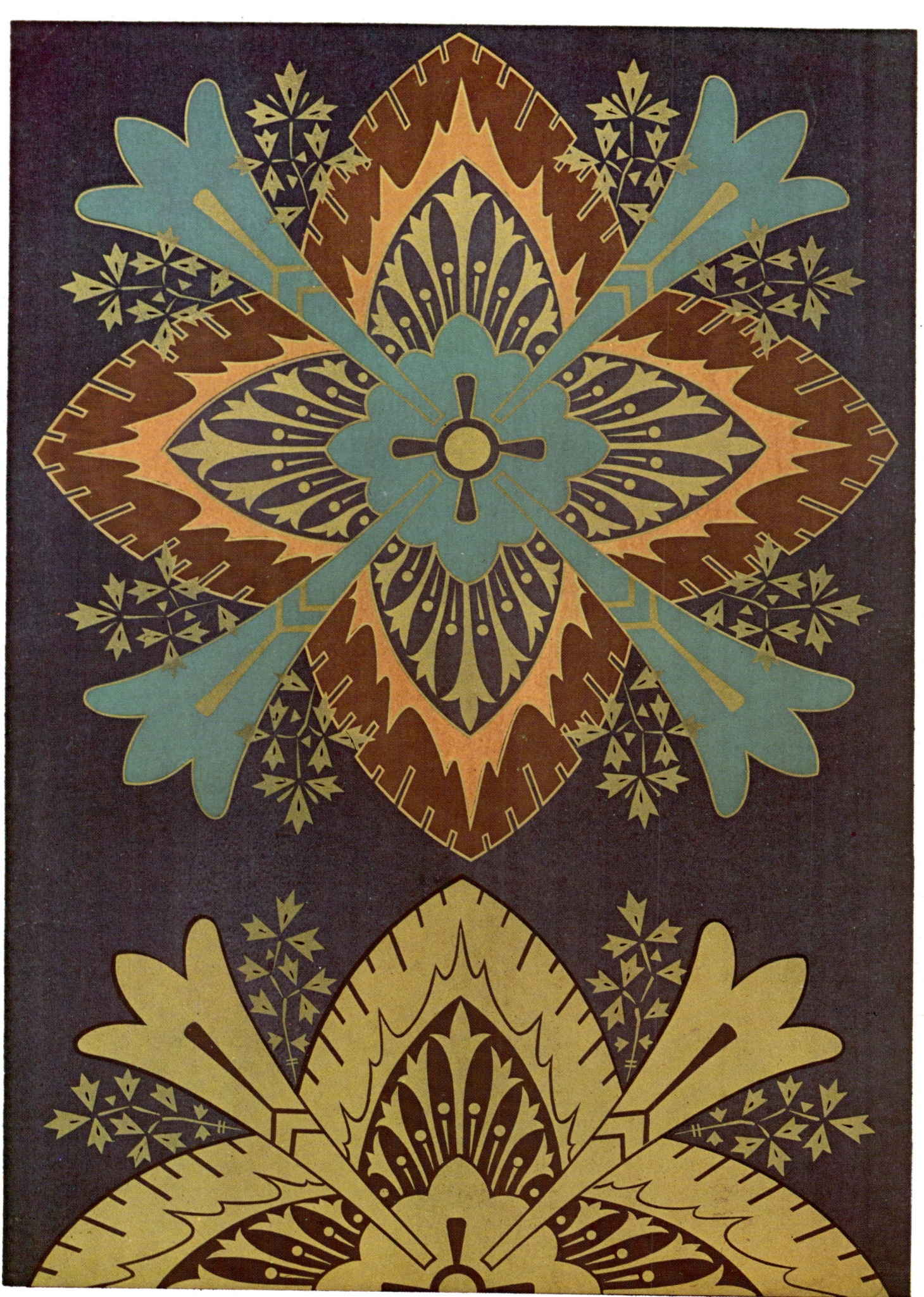

Two color treatments of a ceiling pattern.

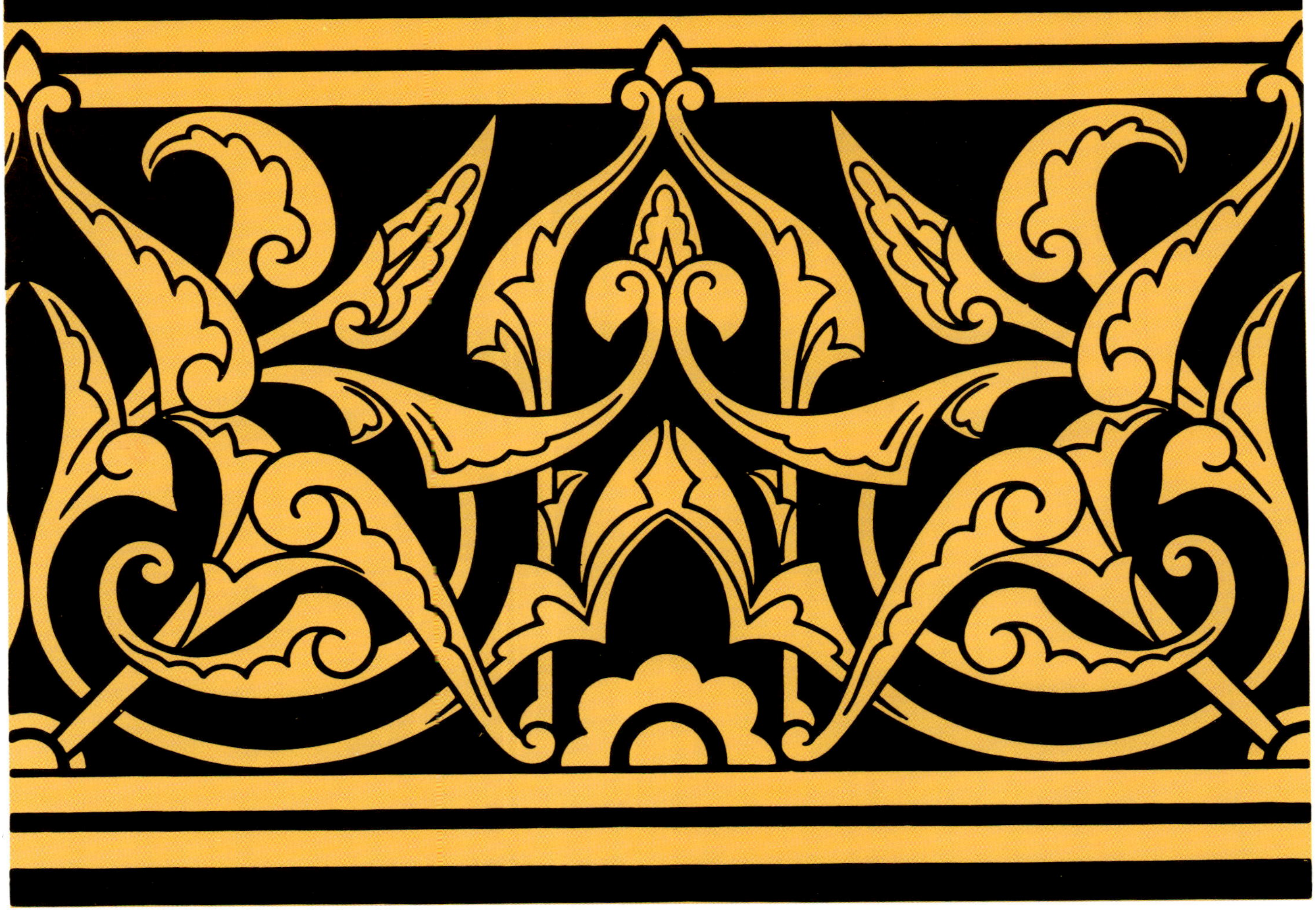

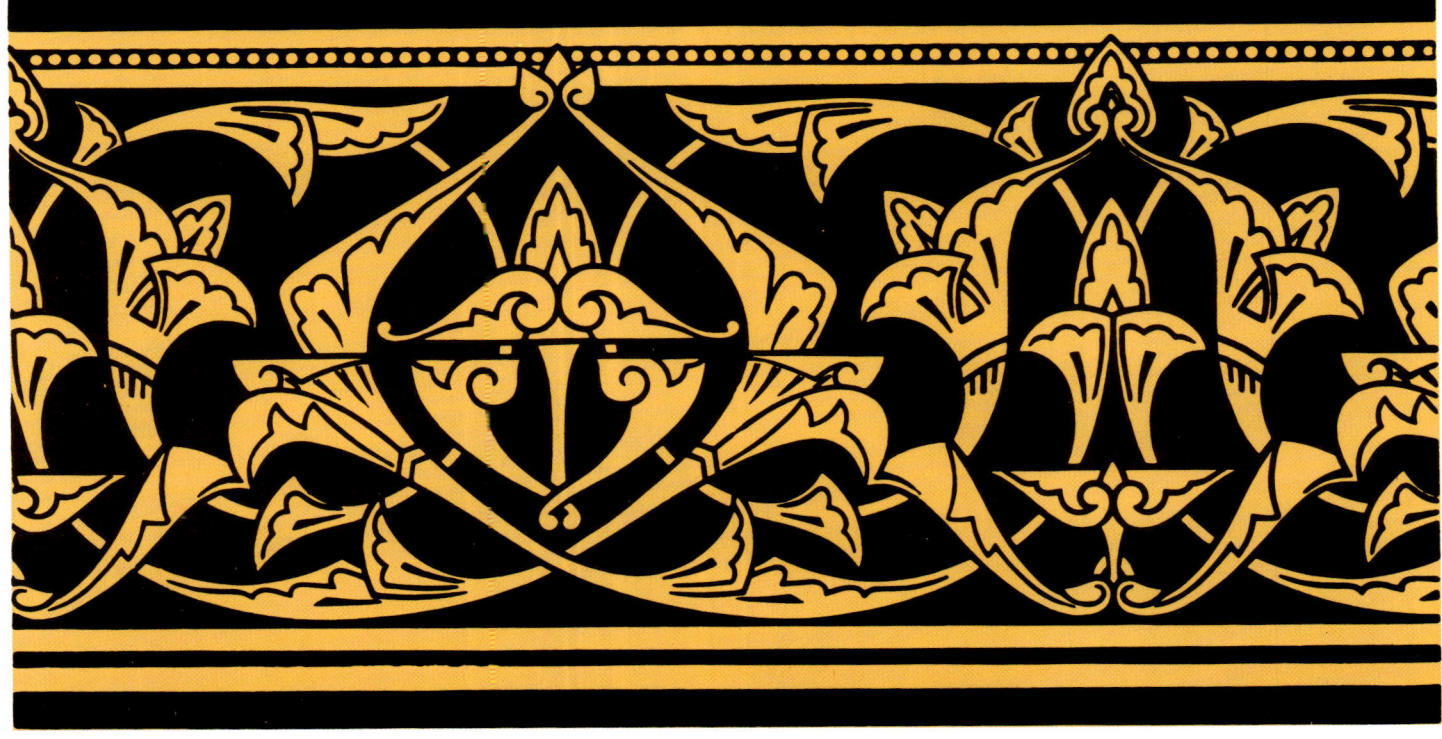

Two dado-rail ornaments in the Arabian style.

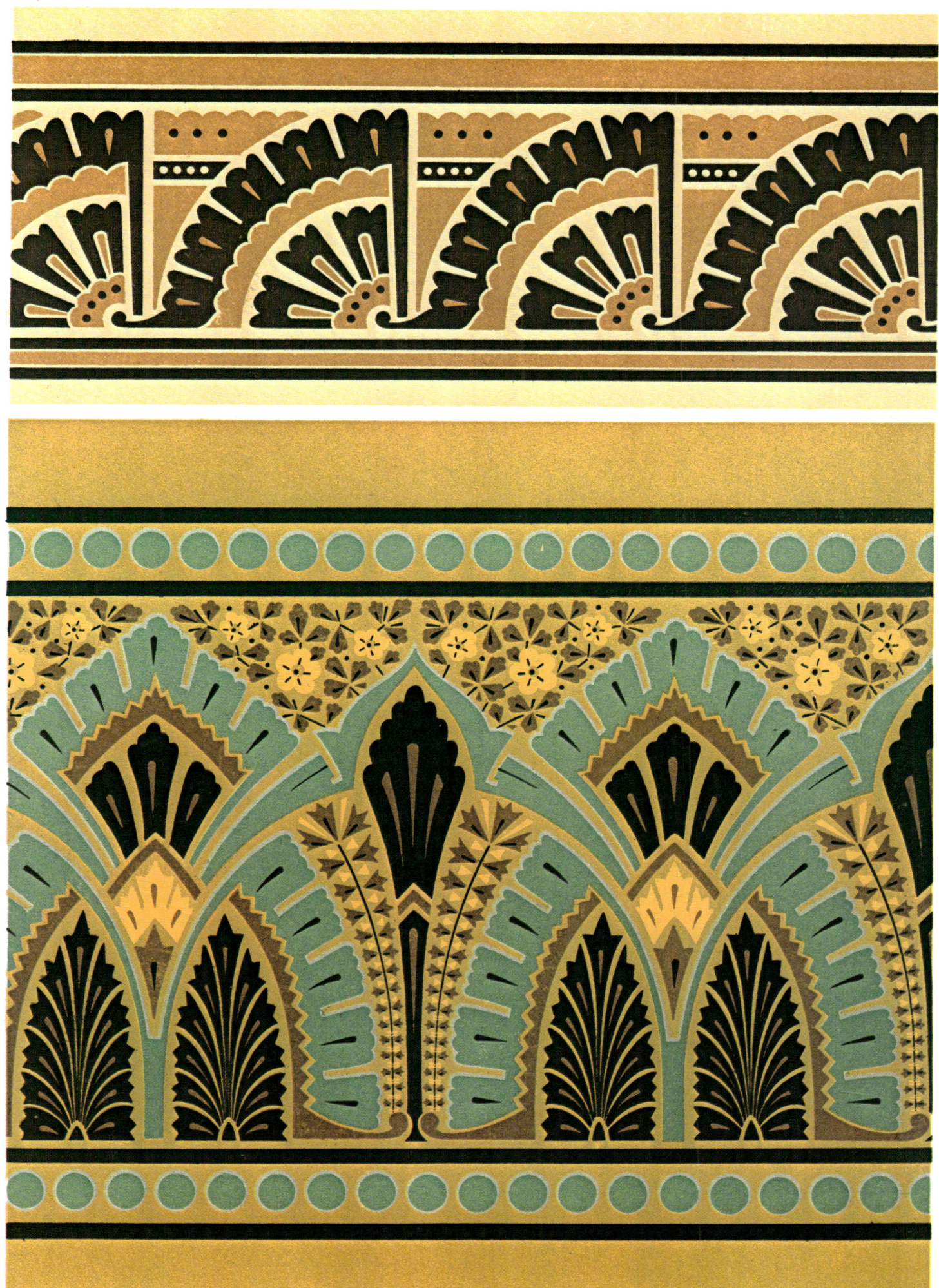

Architectural border ornaments.

Wall pattern.

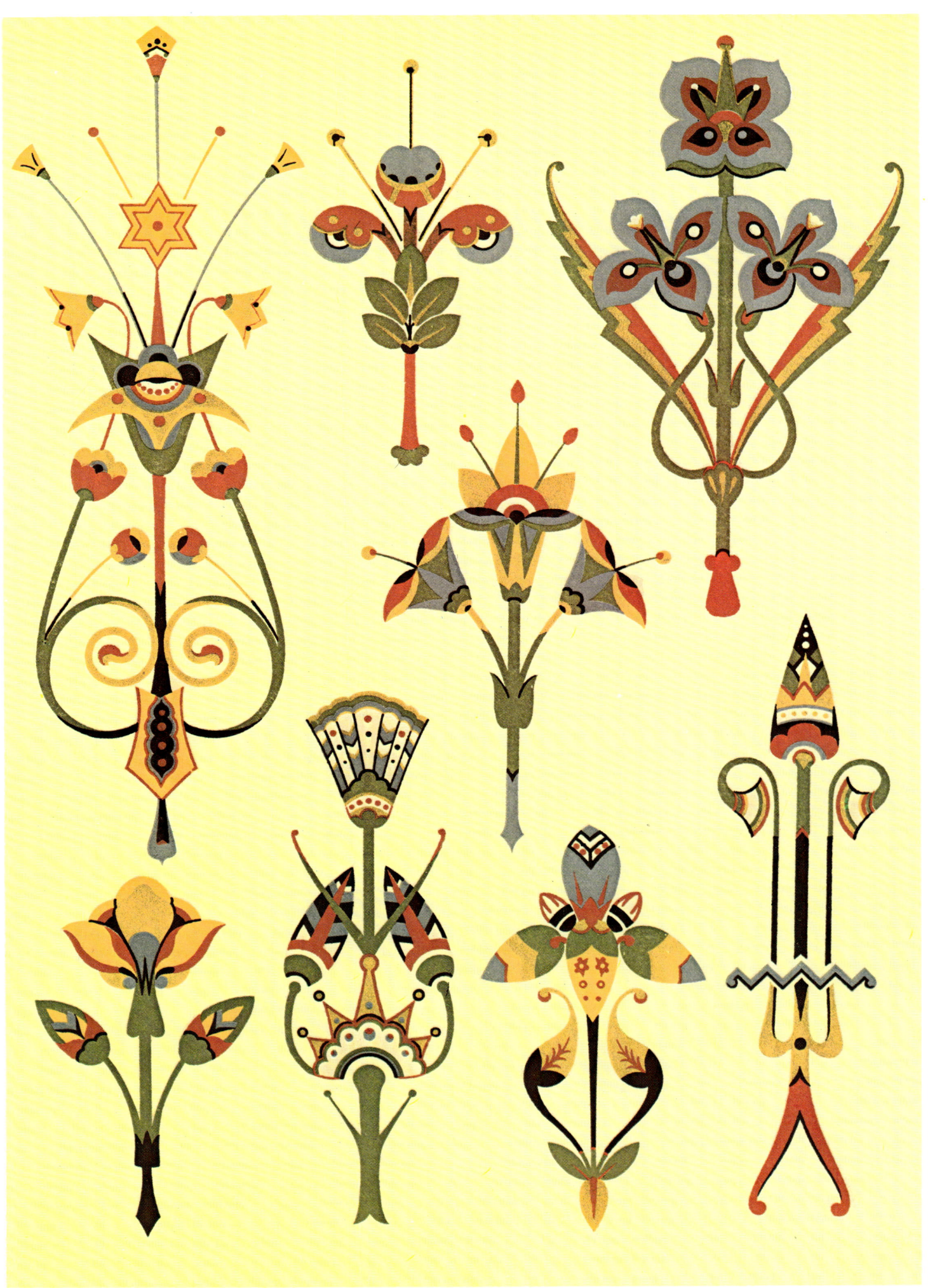

Diaper patterns suitable for stenciling onto walls.

Dado rails.

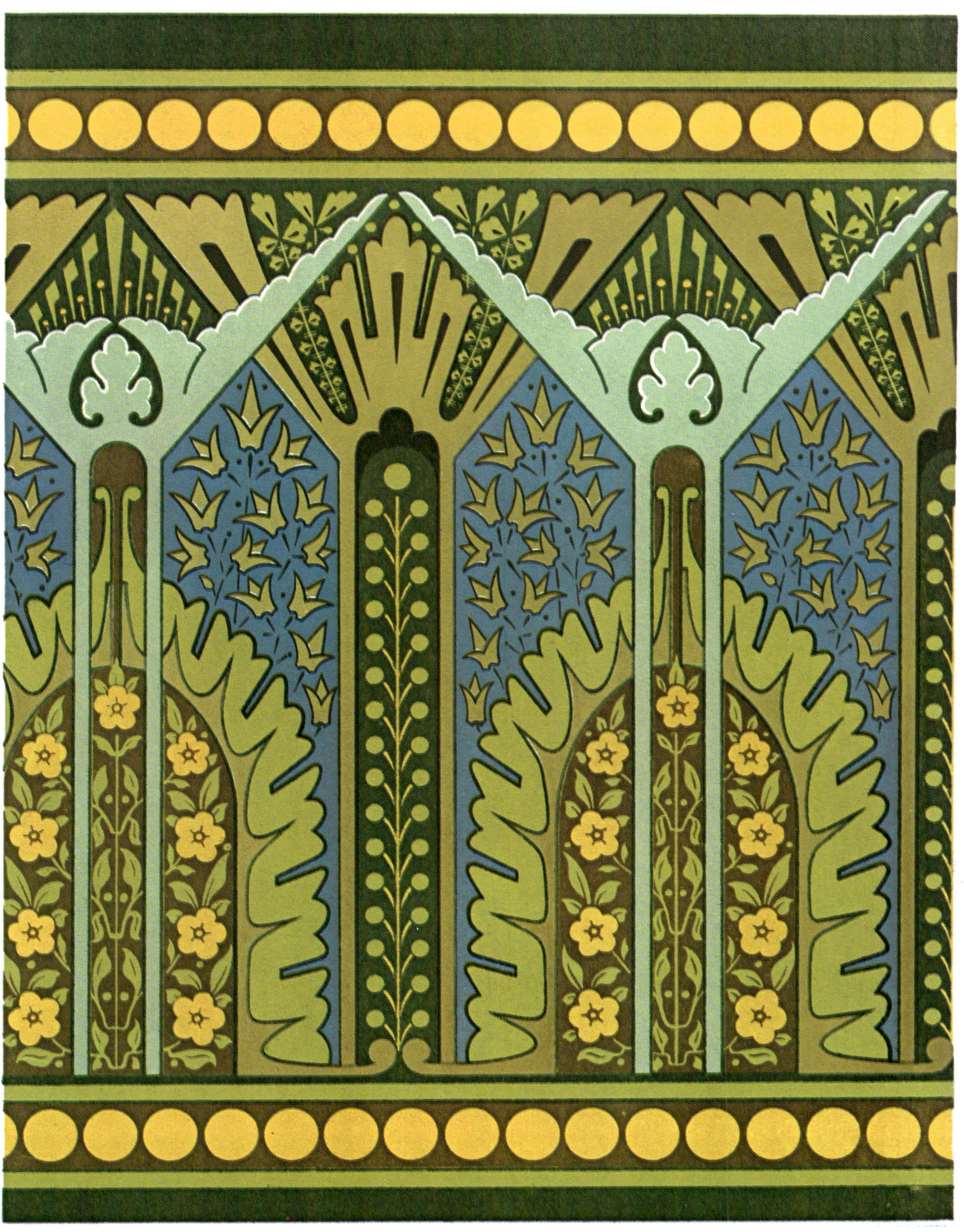

Wall frieze.

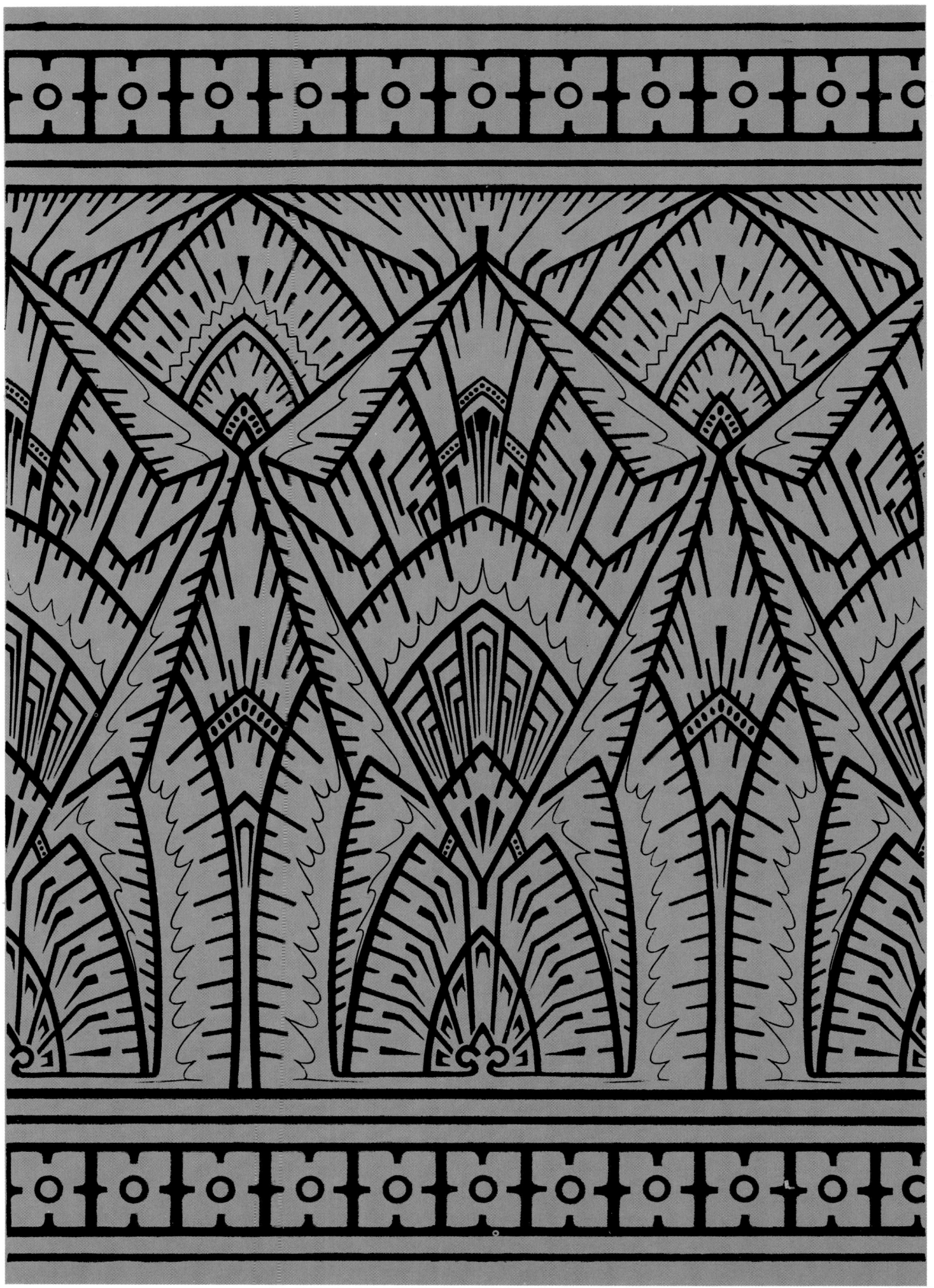
Wall frieze.

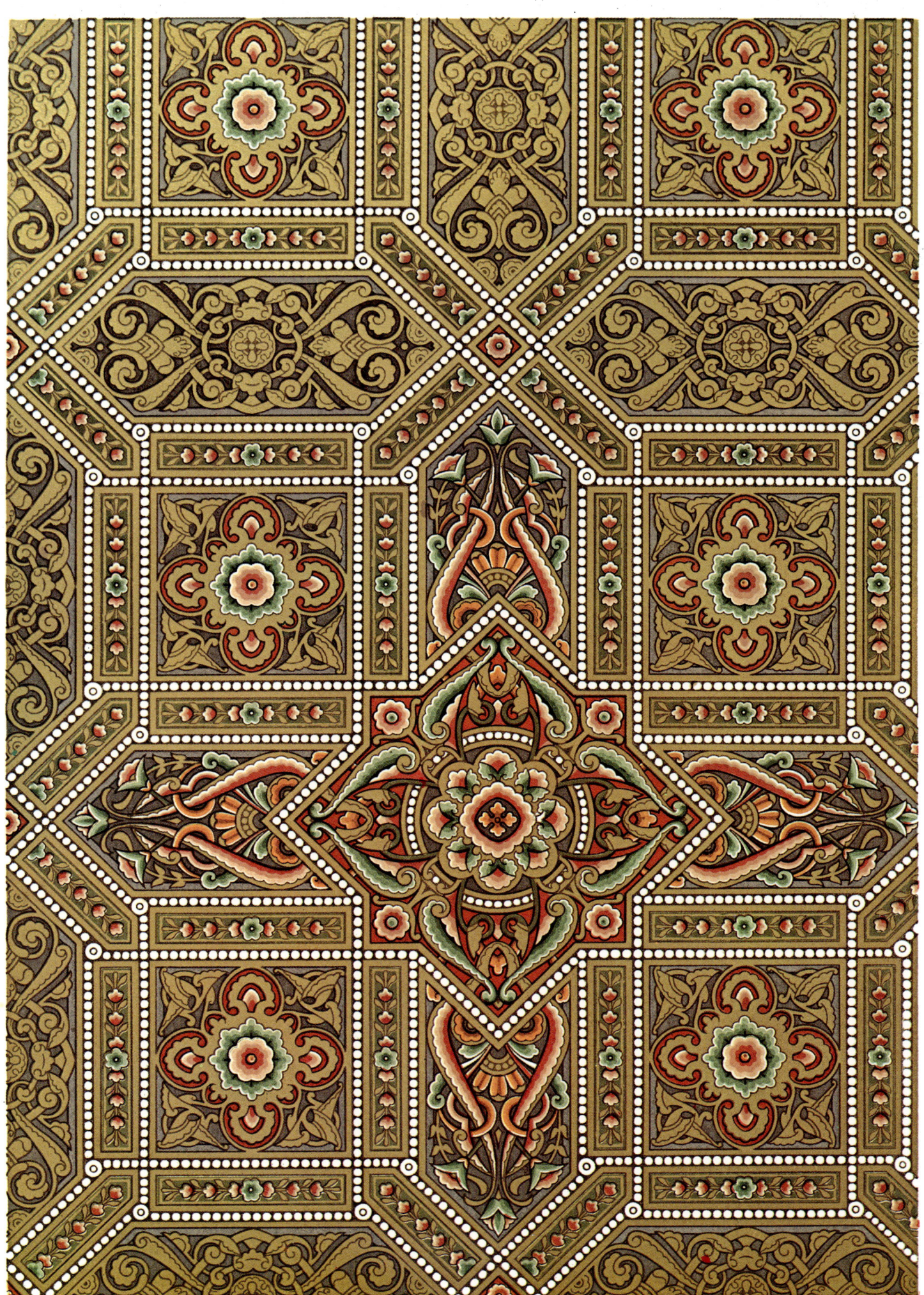
Ceiling ornament.

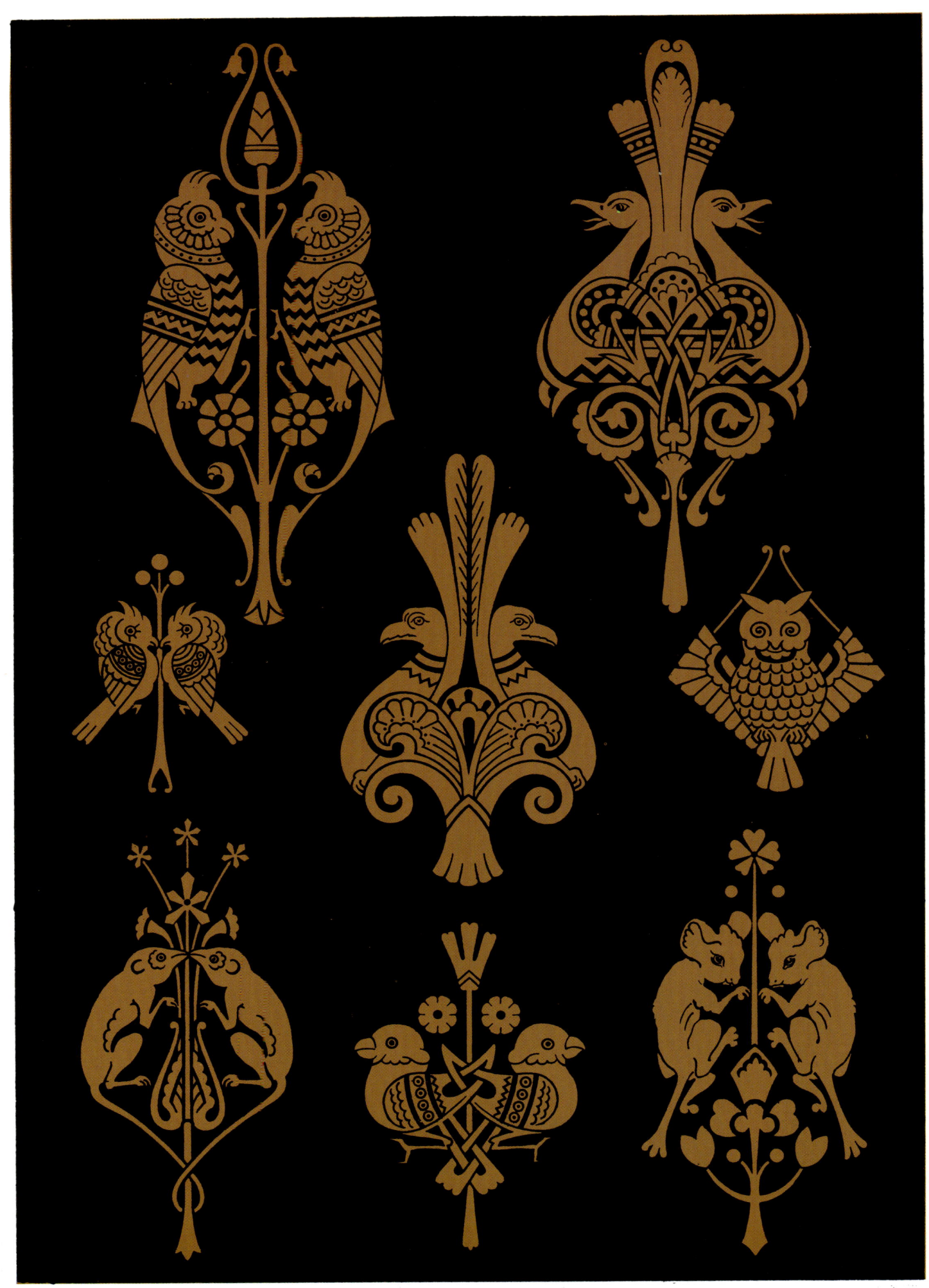
Grotesque powderings (spot ornaments) for walls.

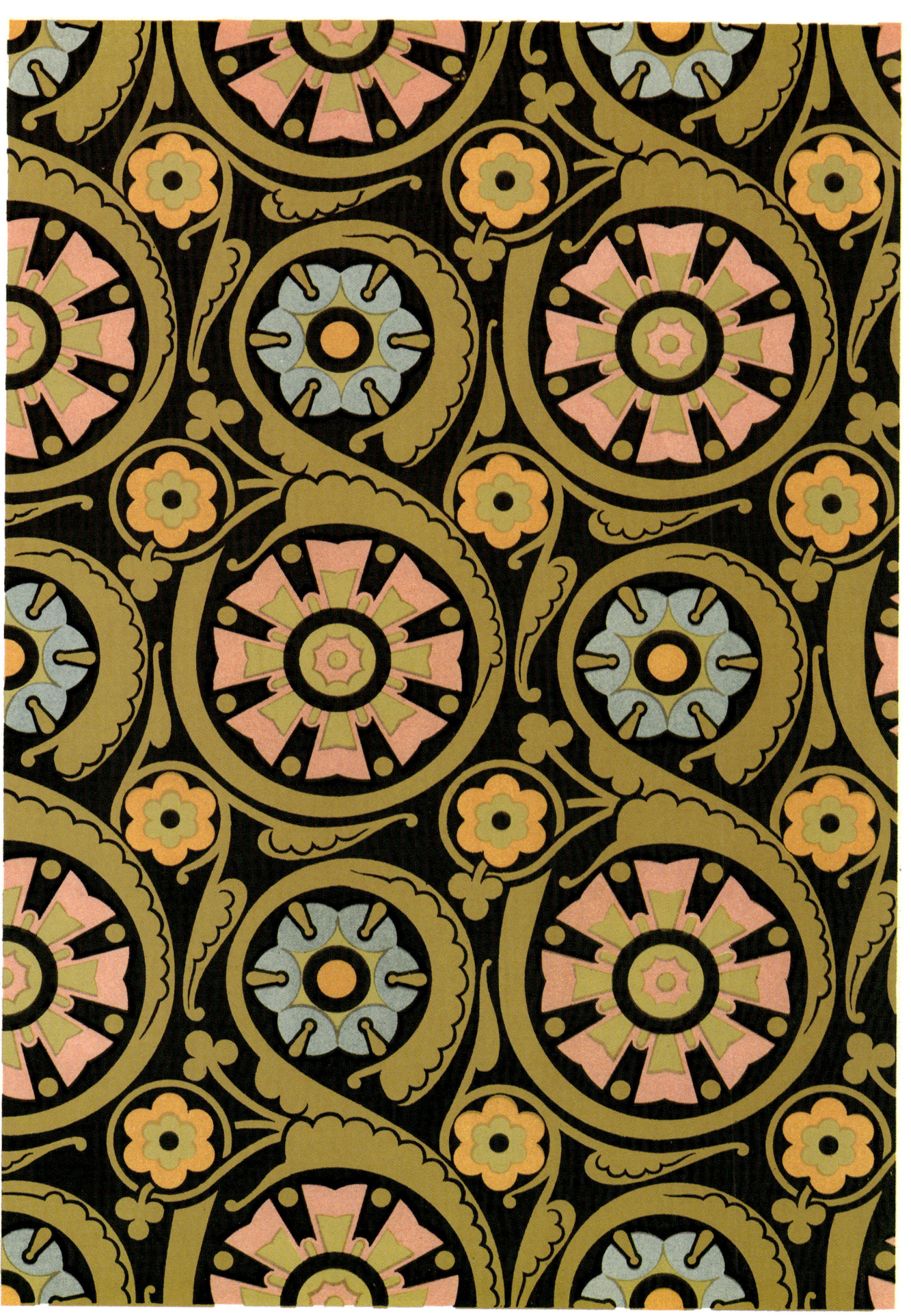

Design for a wall or dado.

Wall or dado ornament.

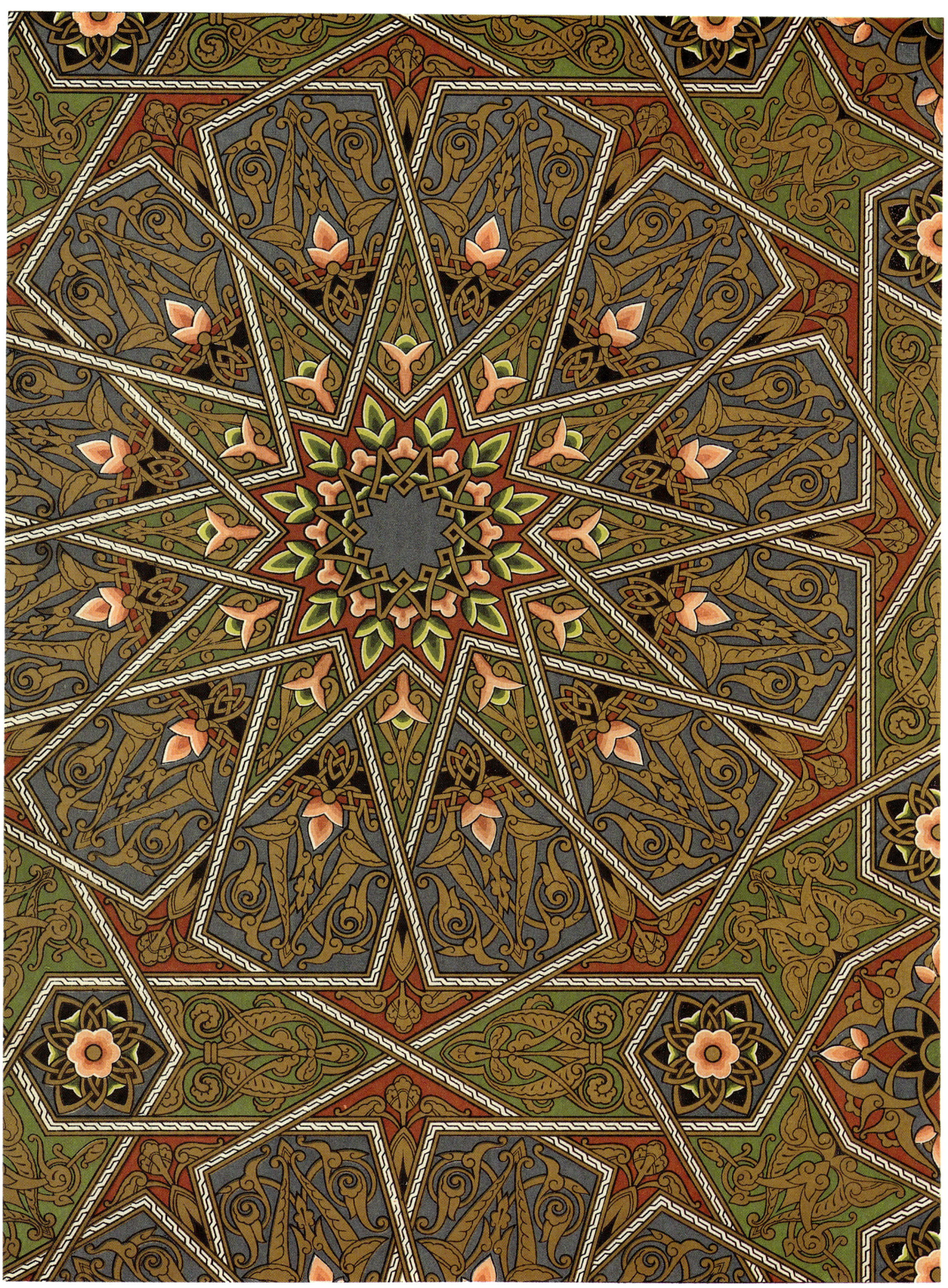

Ceiling ornament in the Arabian style.

Wall or dado pattern.

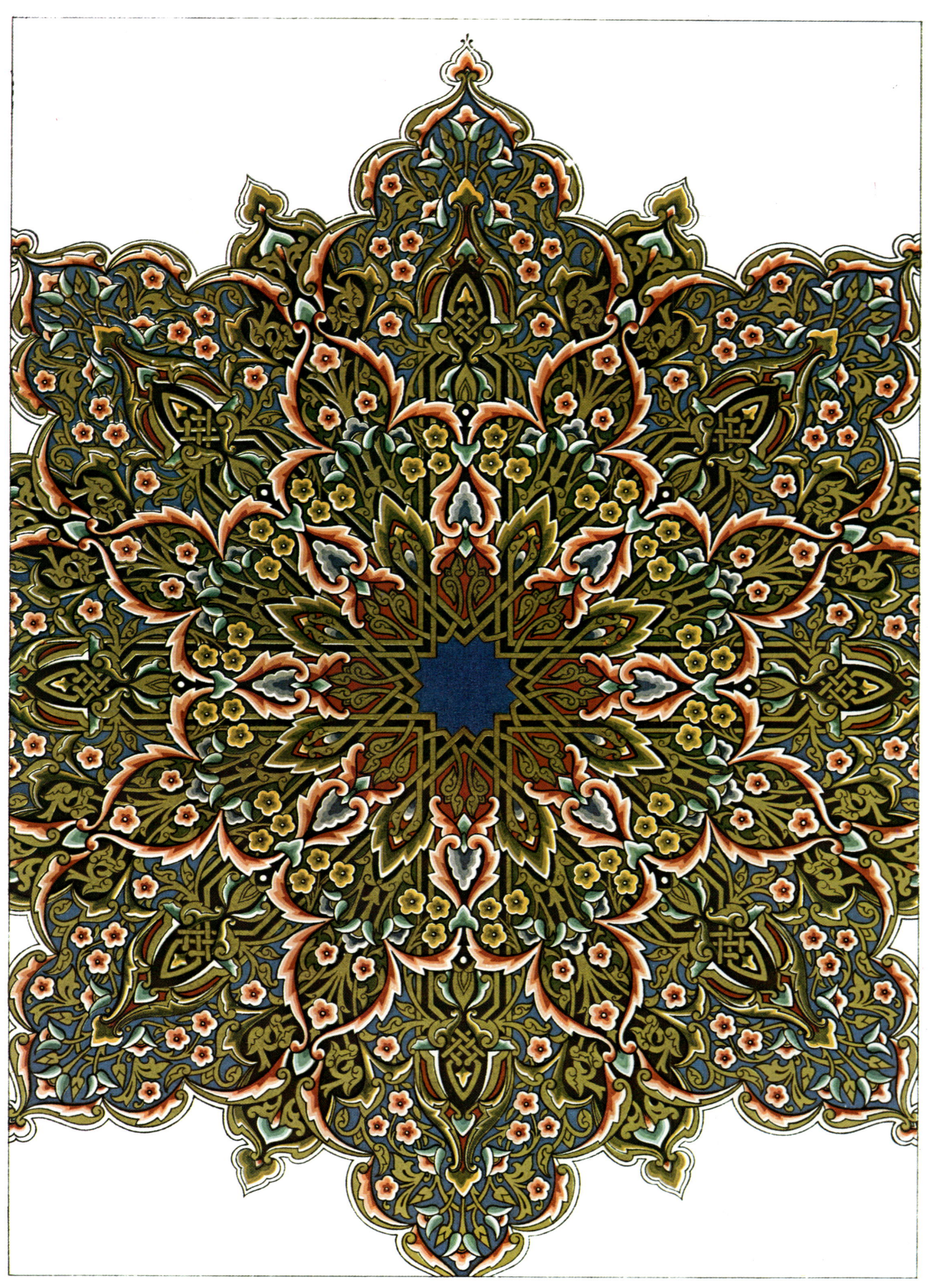

Design in the Arabian style for the central ornament of a ceiling.

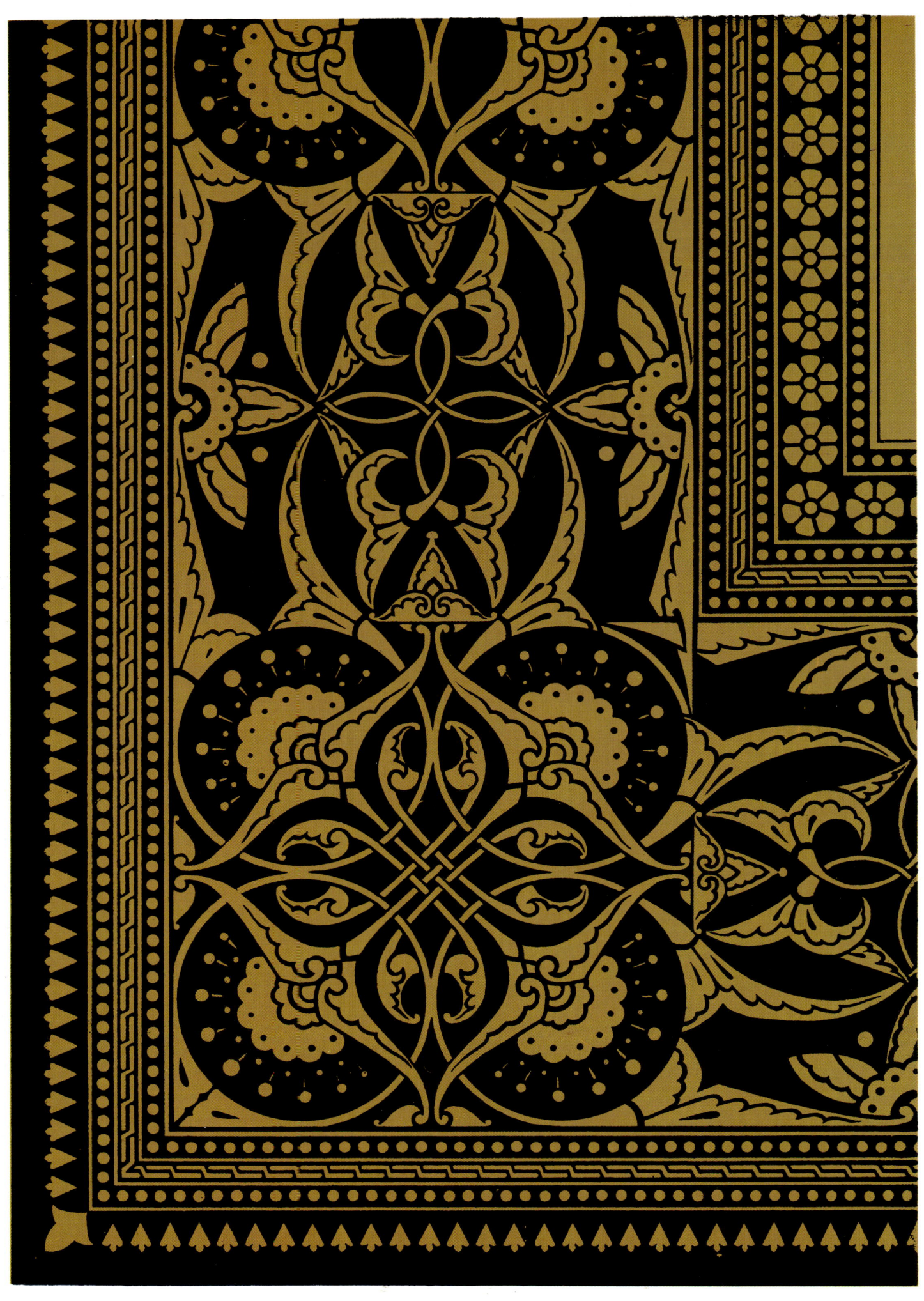

Border with corner for a wall.

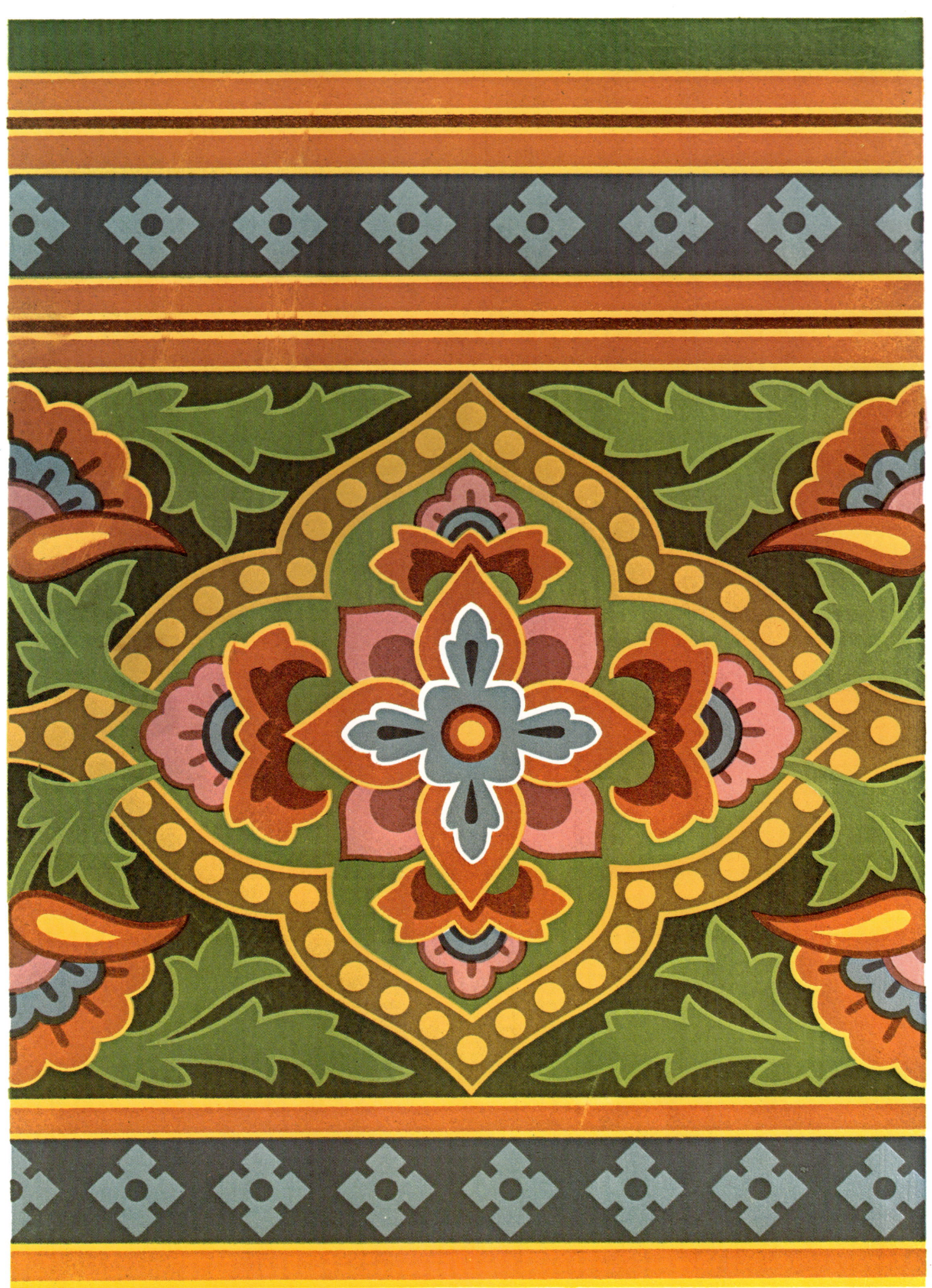

Design for a frieze.

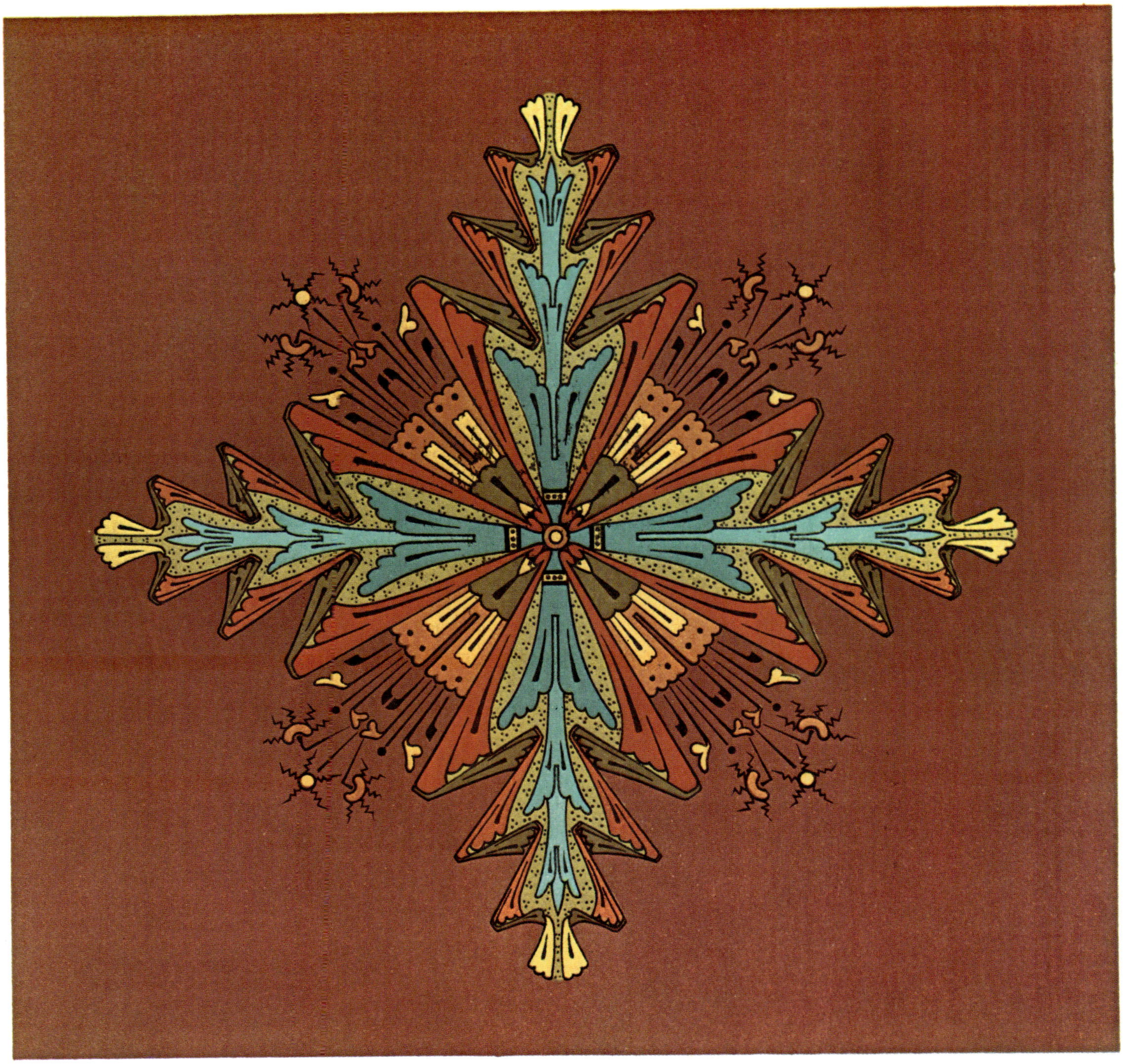

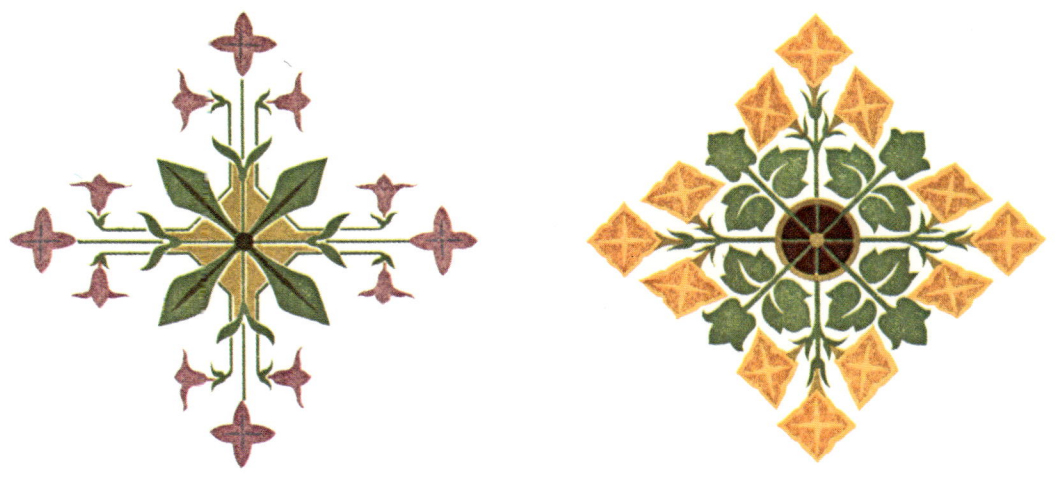

Powderings for dadoes or walls.

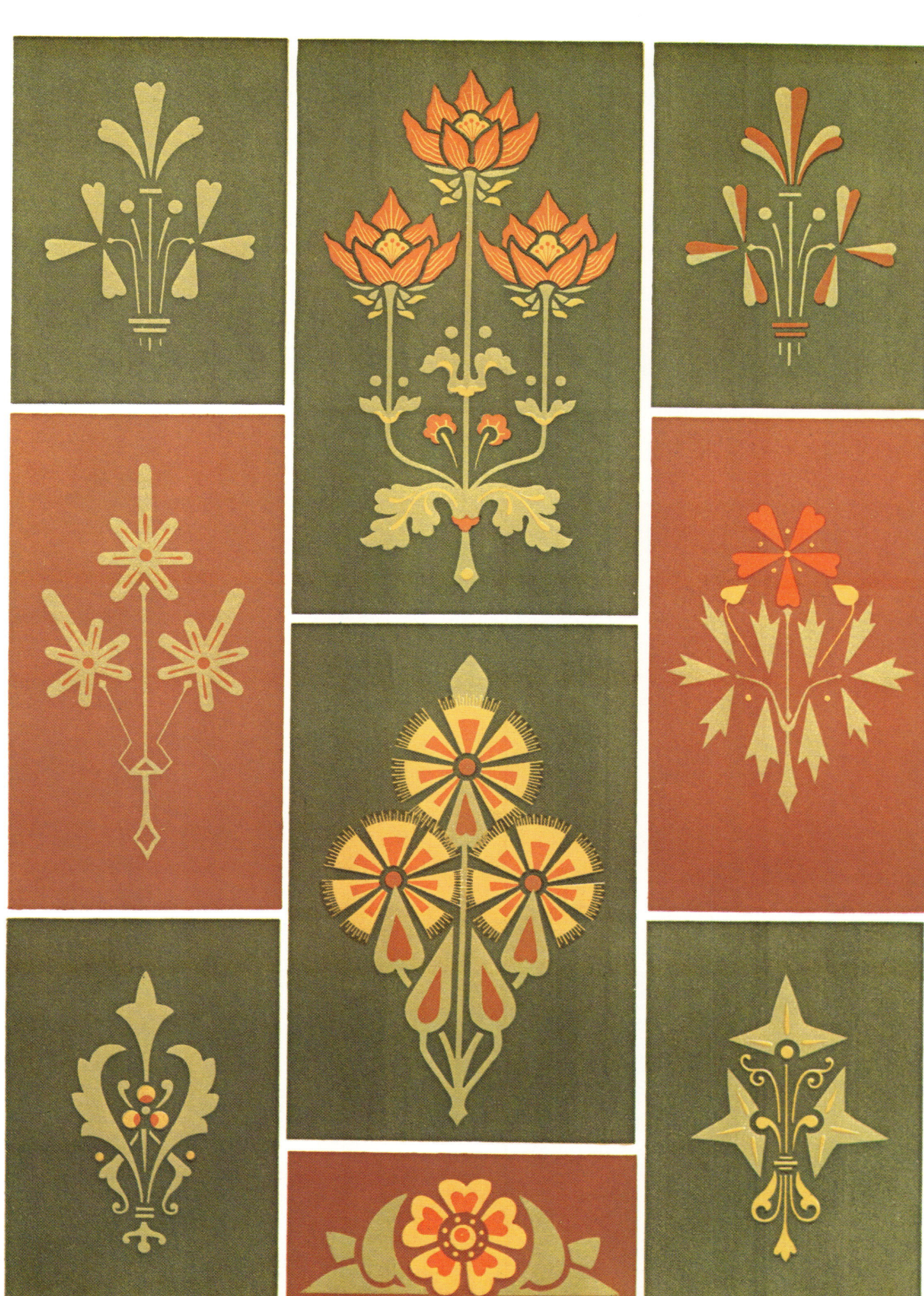
Powderings adapted for wall ornaments.

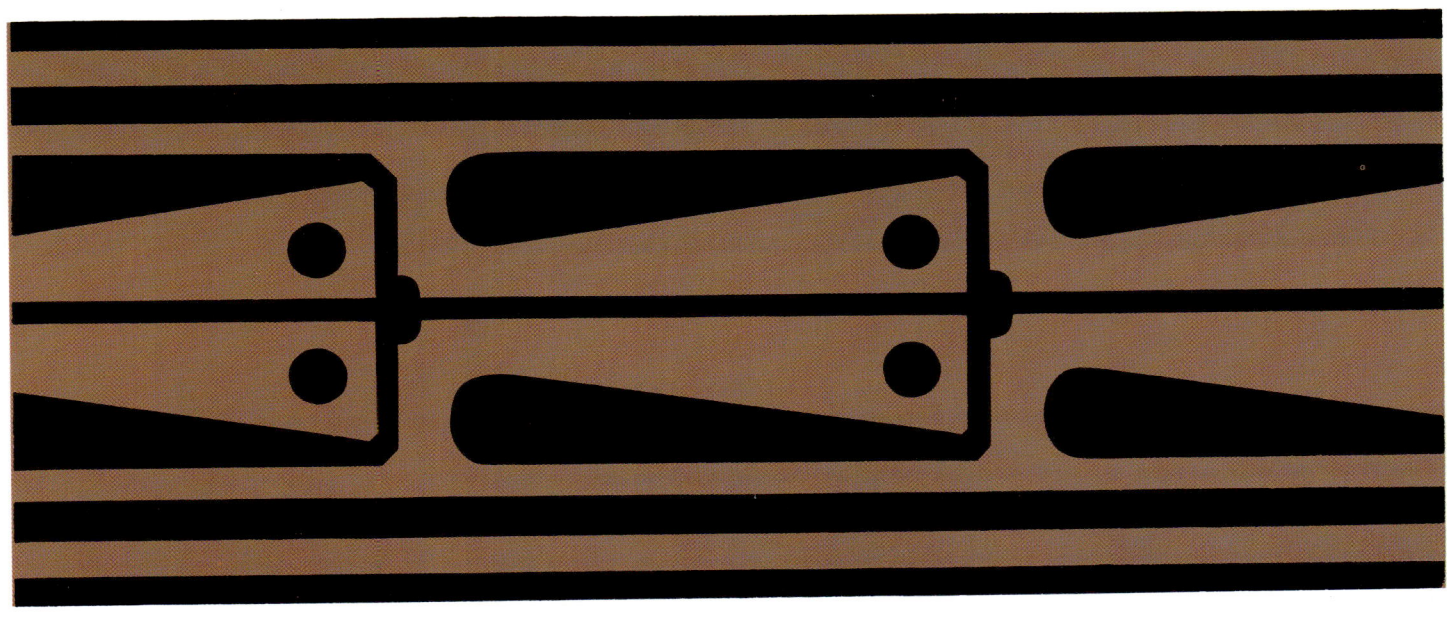
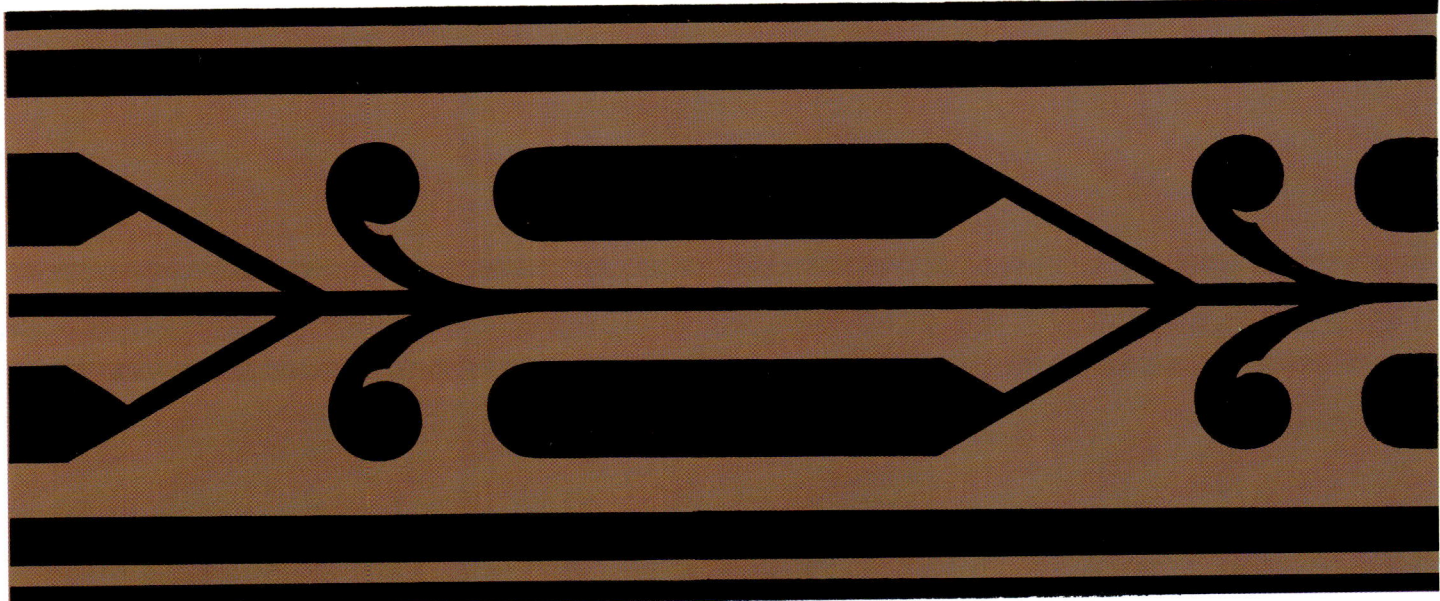
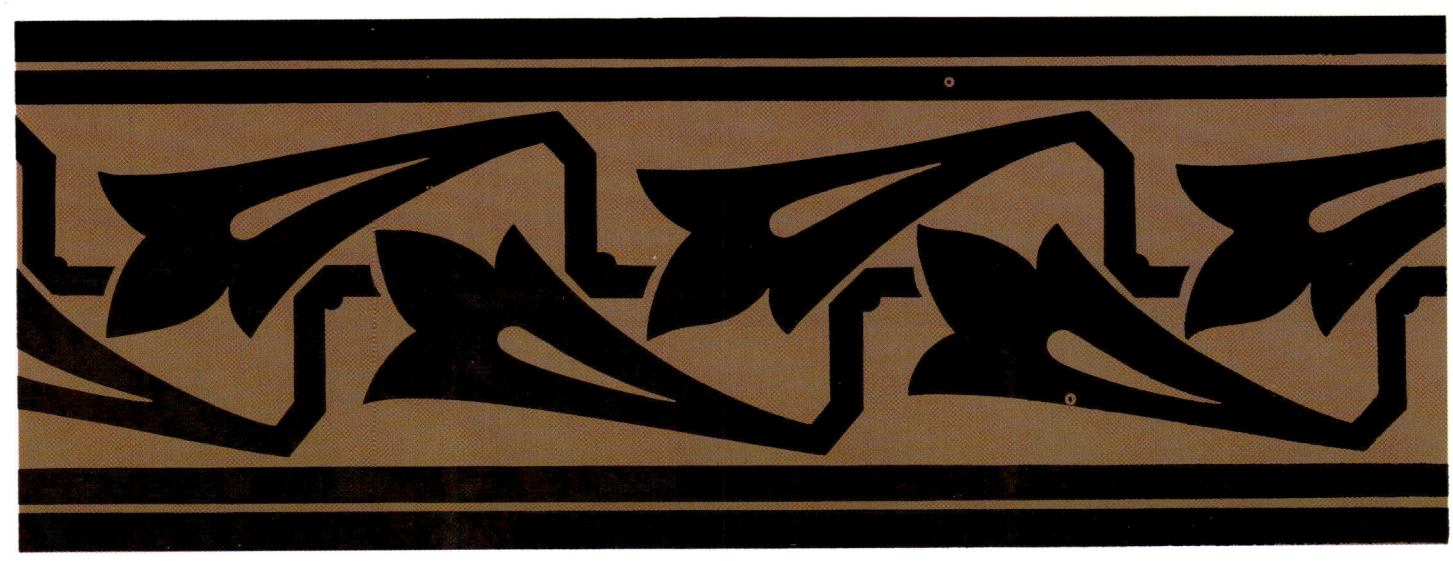

Architectural borderings.

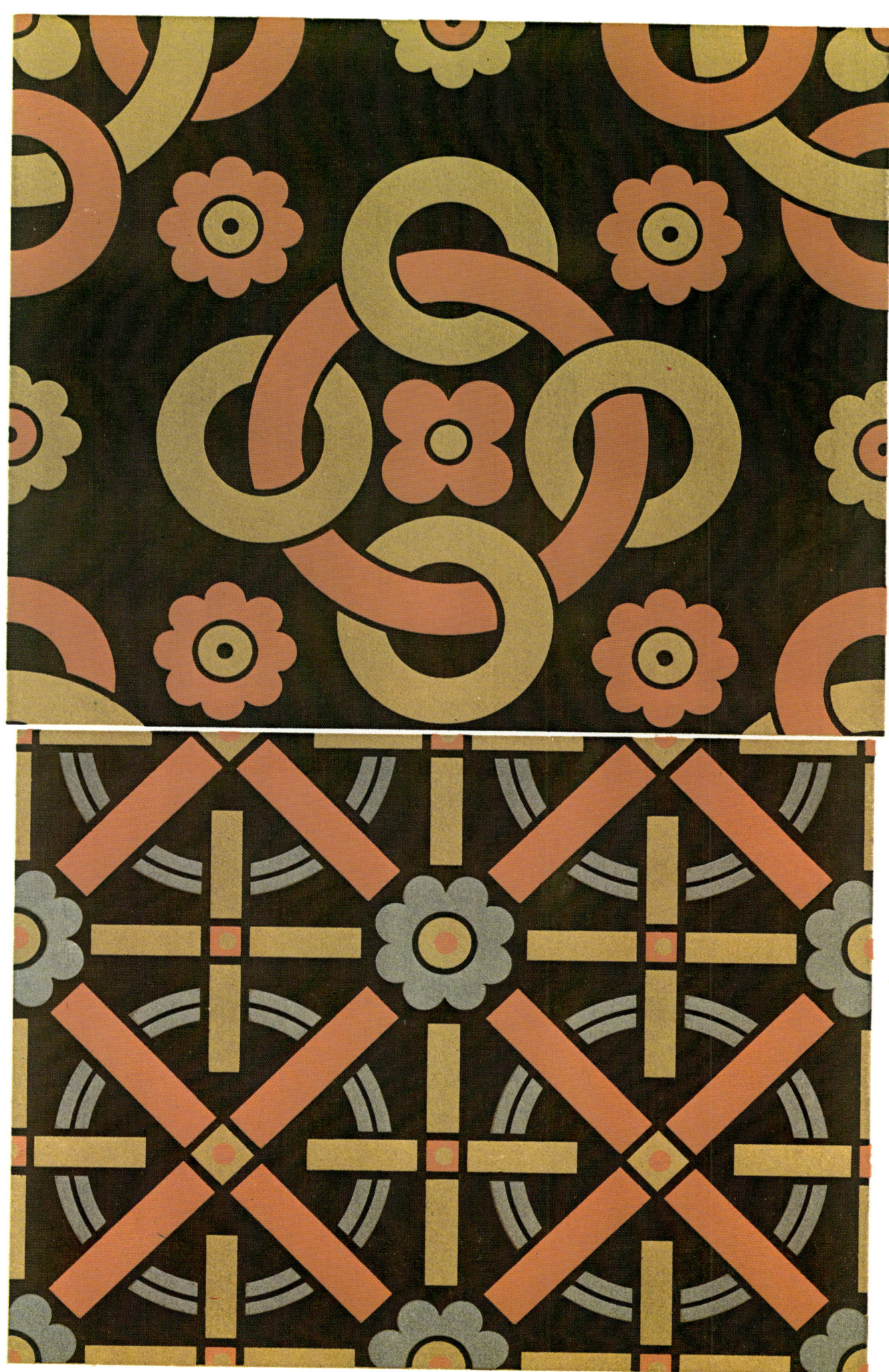
Two patterns for dadoes.

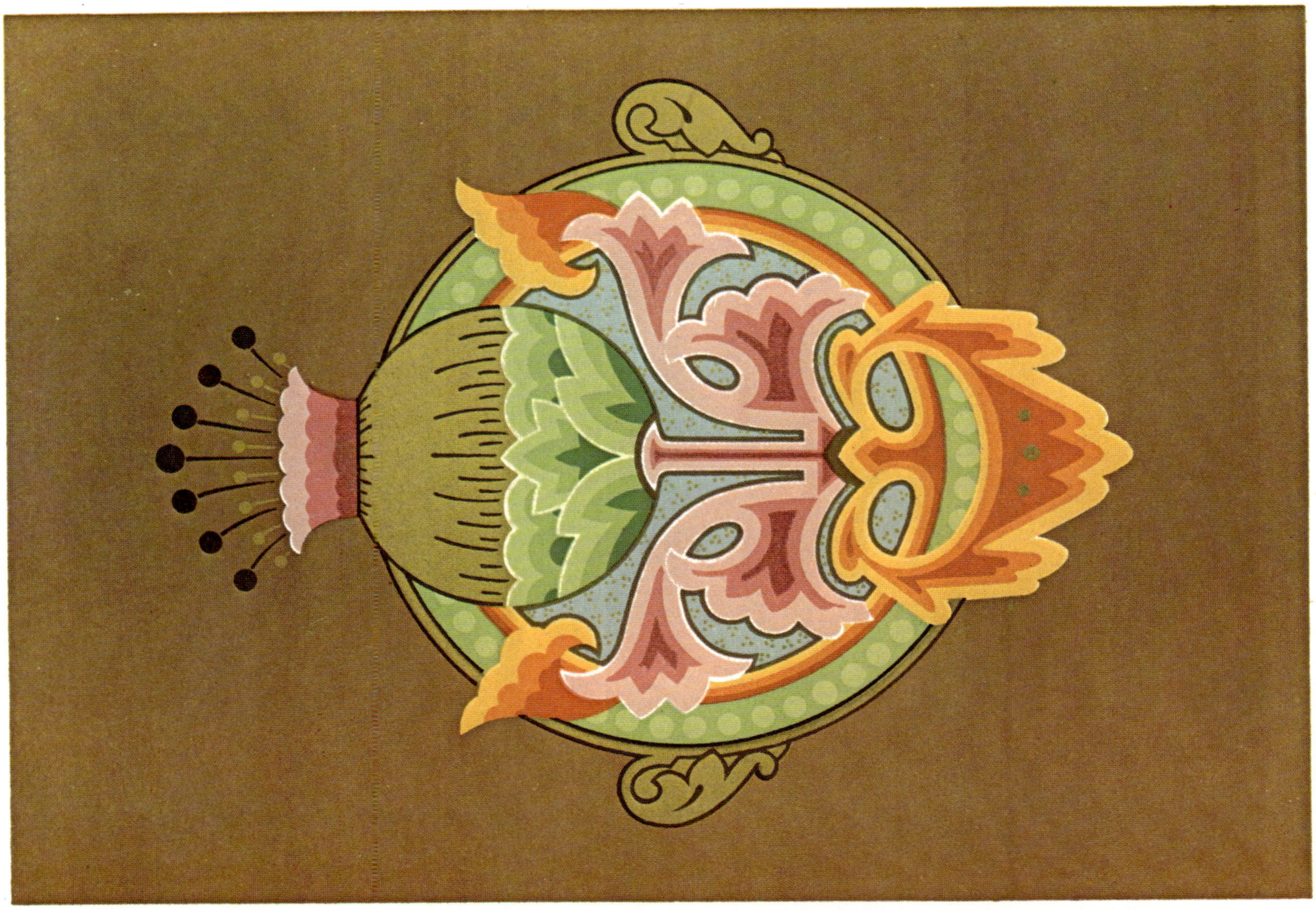

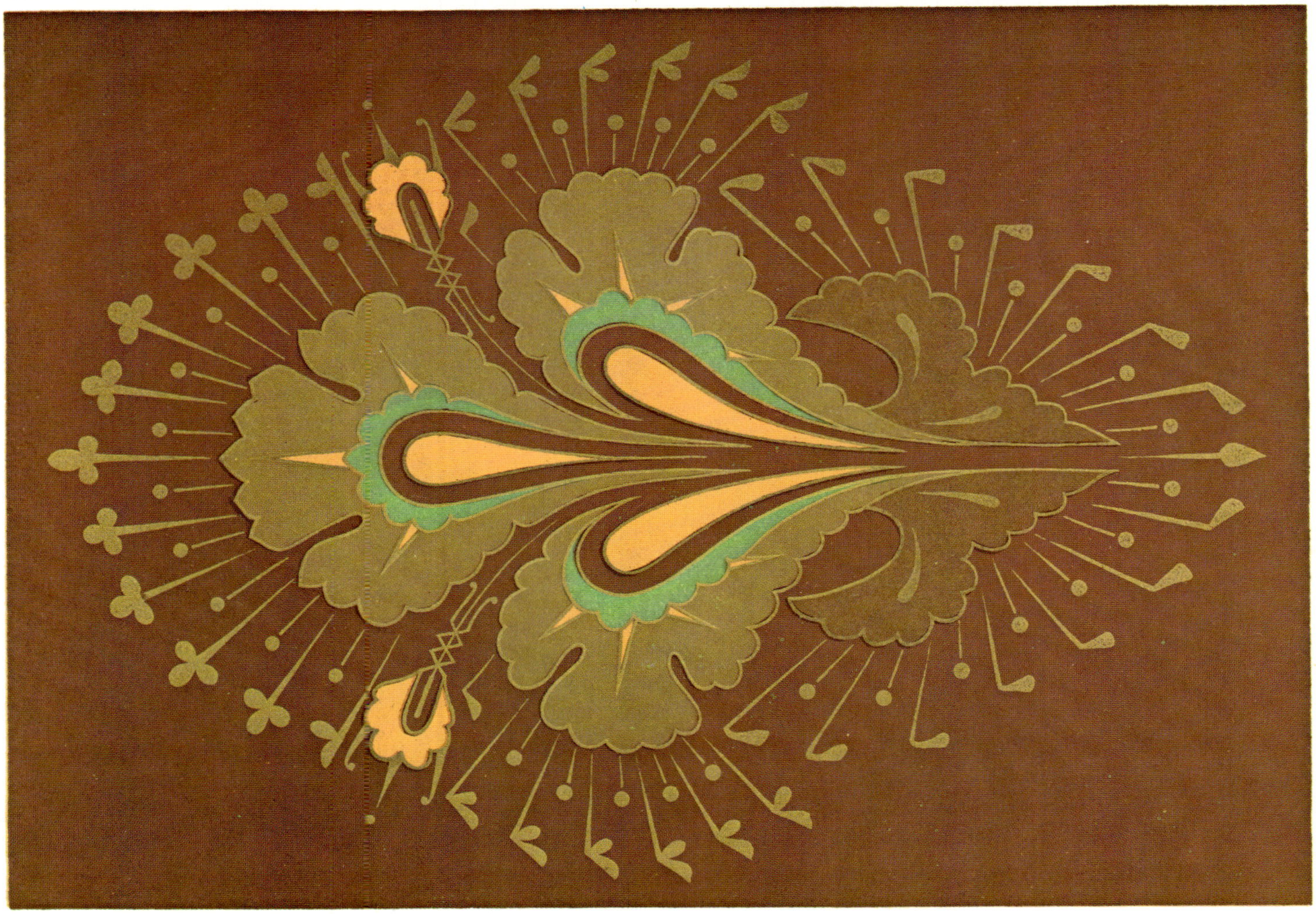

Ornaments for the centers of panels.

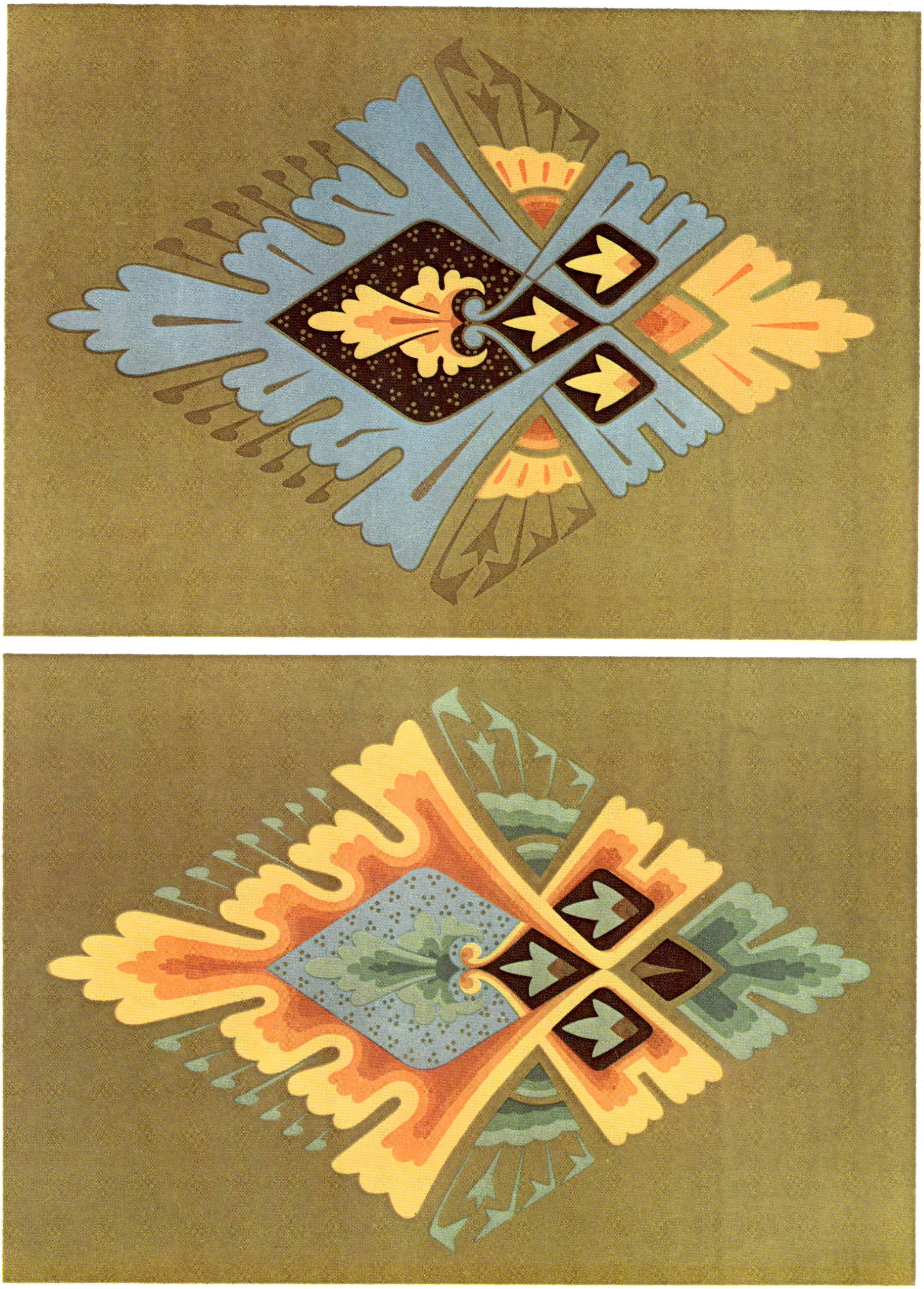

Two color treatments of an ornament suitable for a panel.

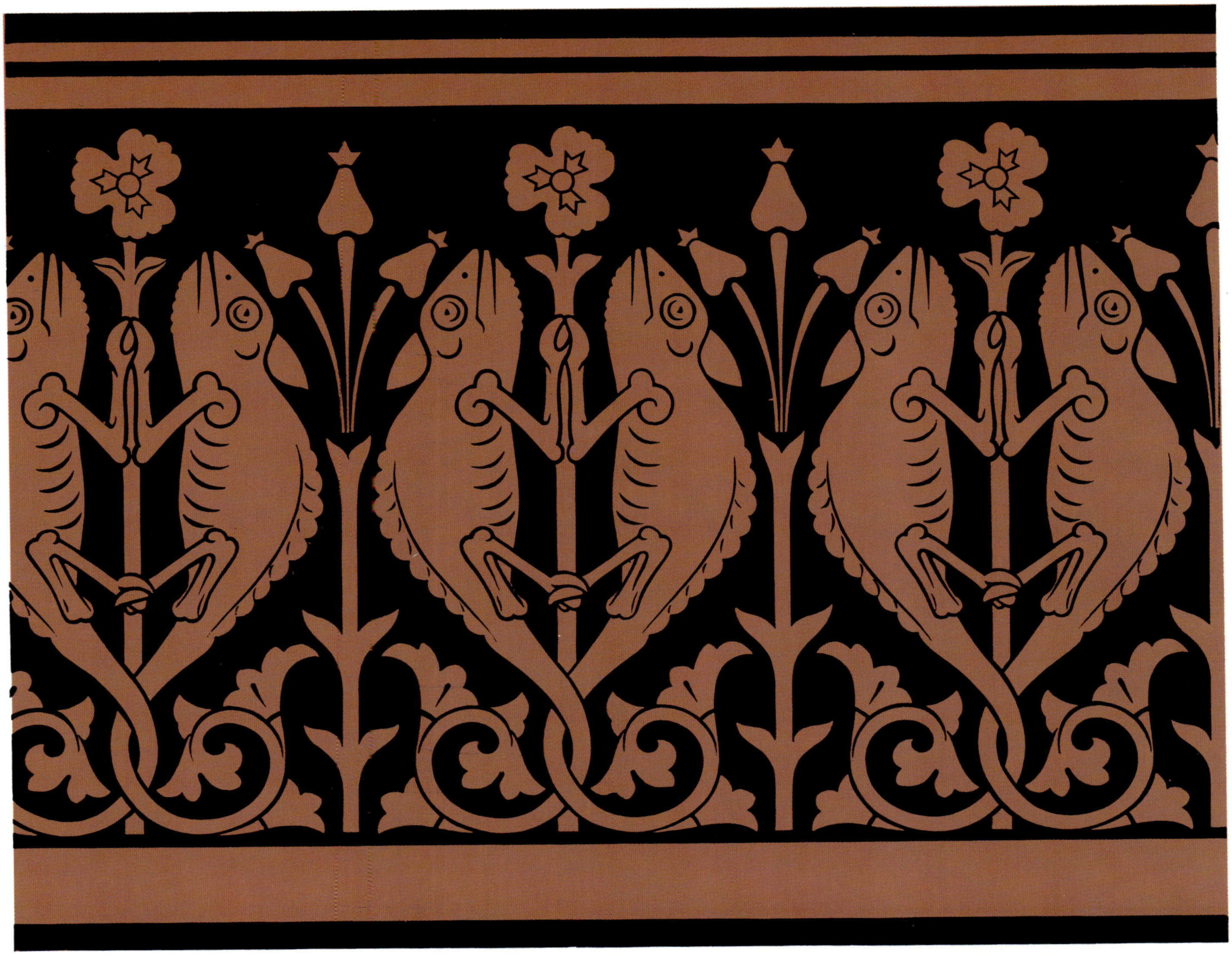

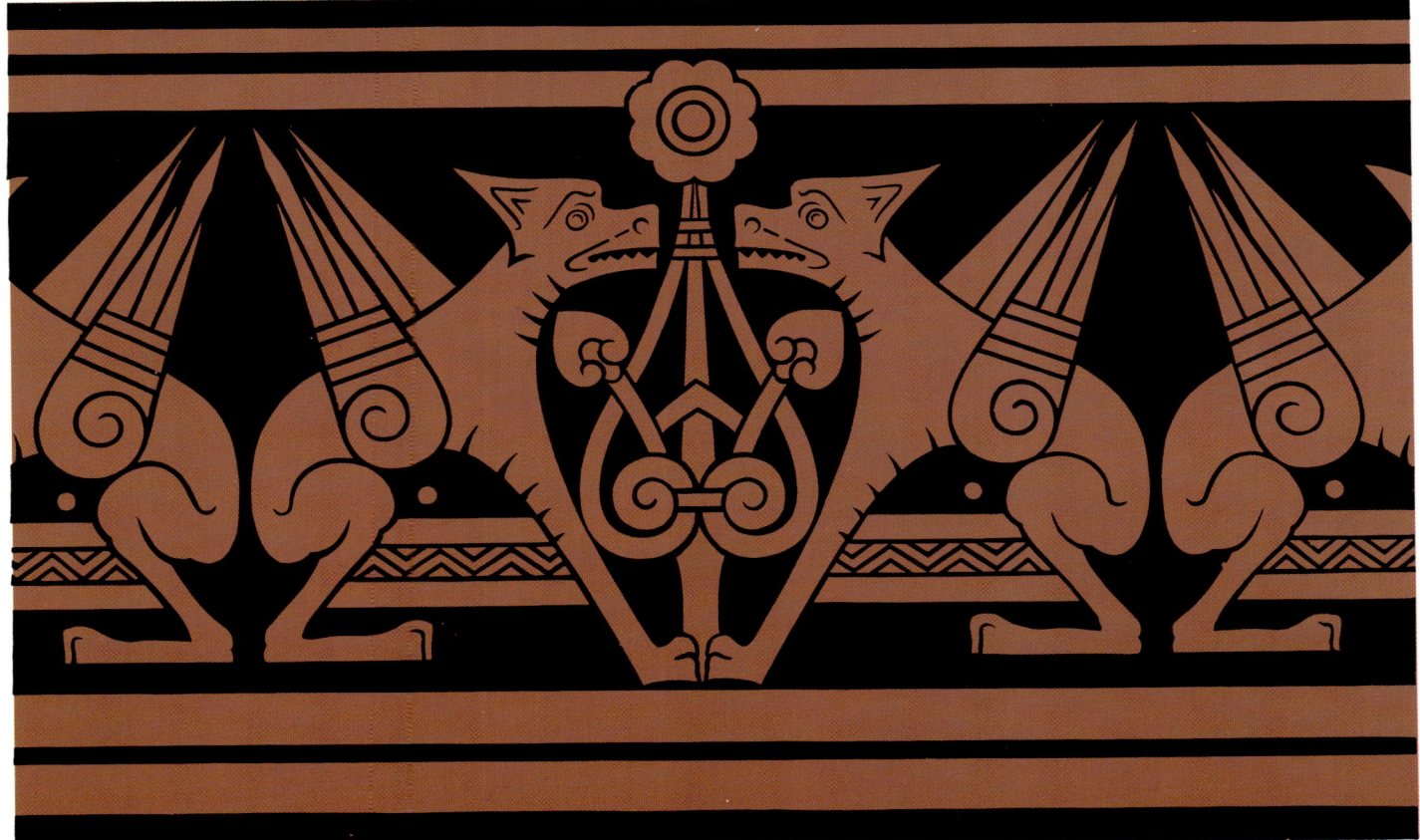

Two grotesque dado rails.

Dado rails or frieze ornaments.

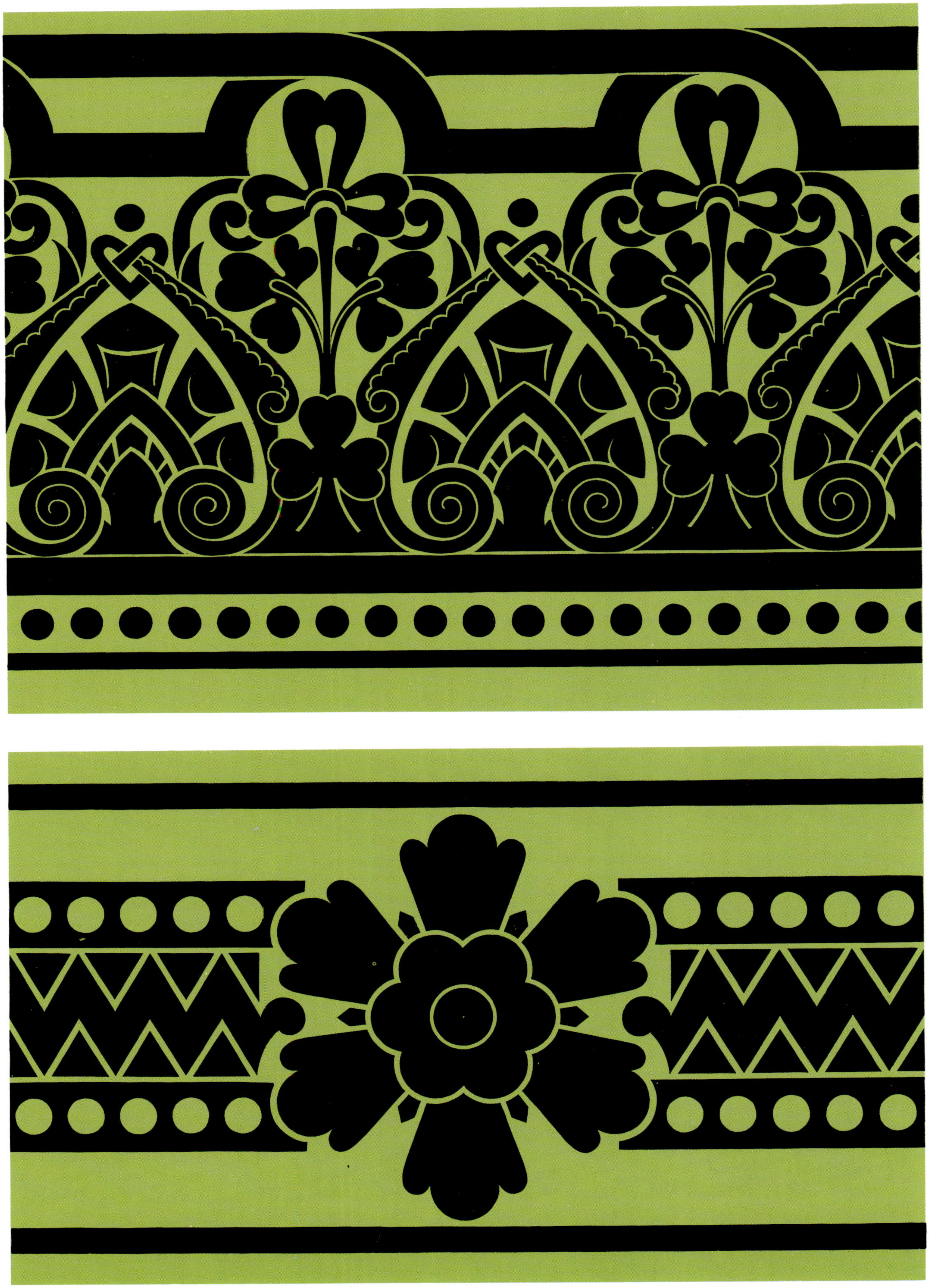

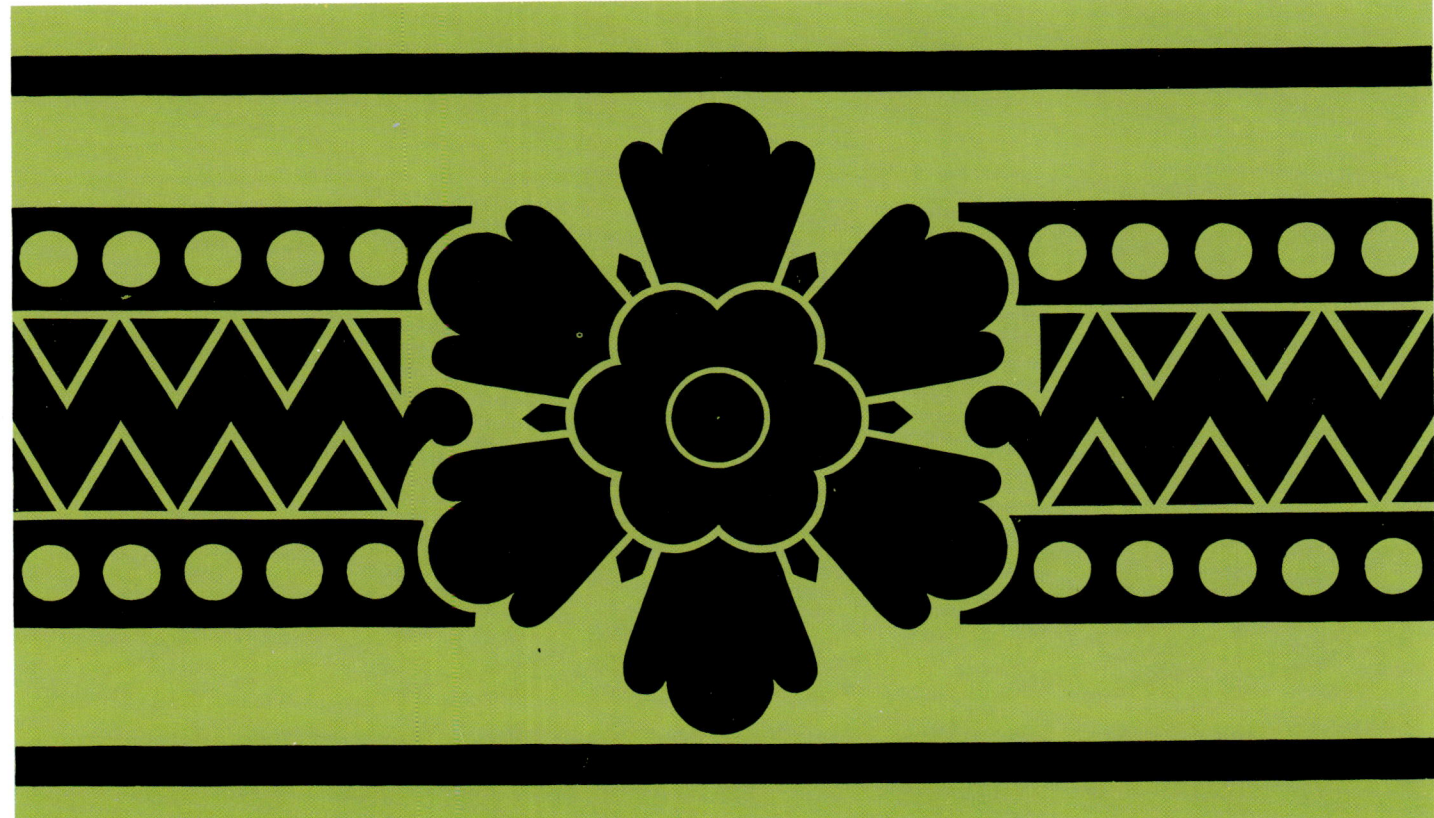

Ornaments for friezes or dado borderings.

Allover pattern for a wall.

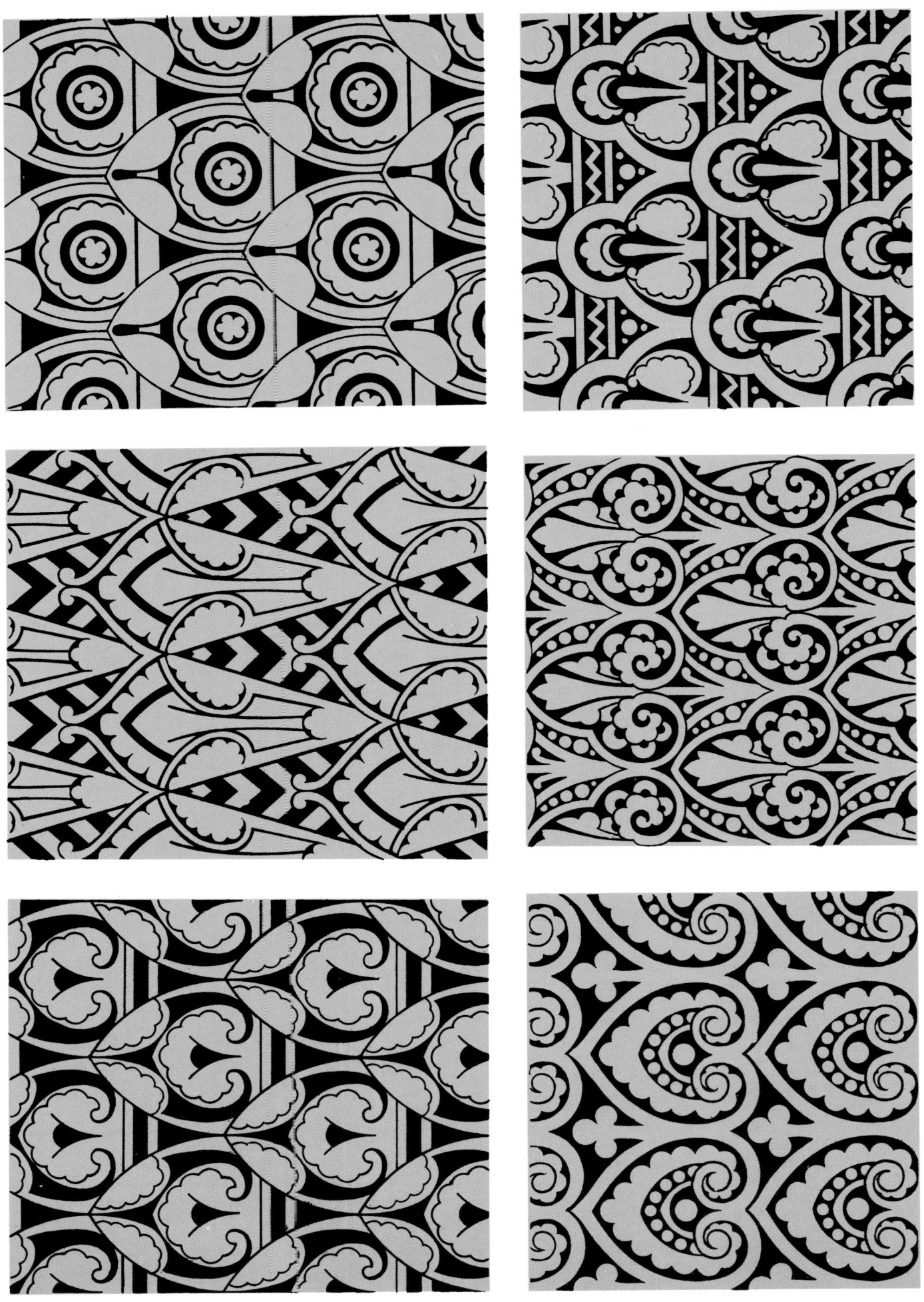

Diaper patterns for dadoes.

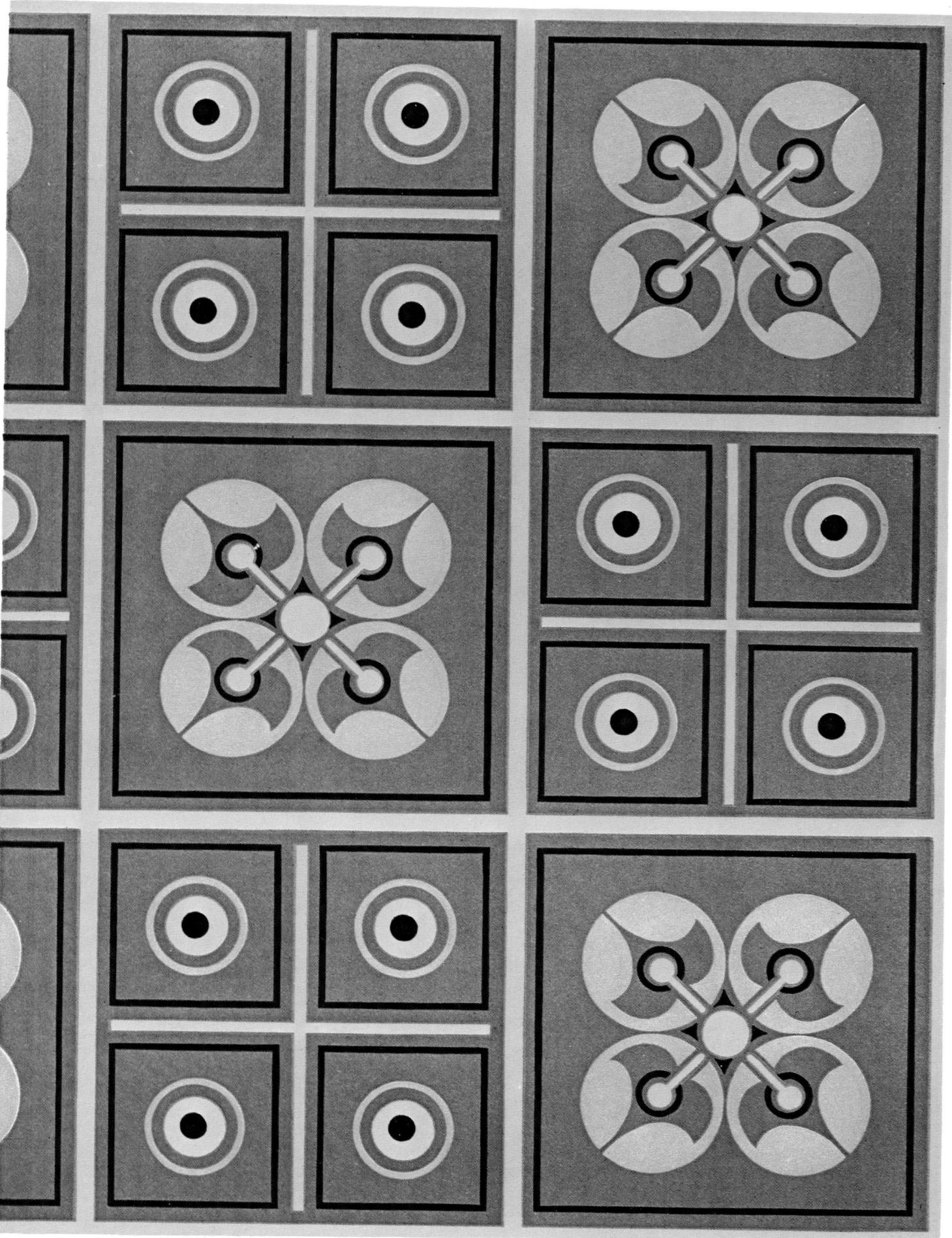

Dado ornament.

Ornament for the top of a dado rail.

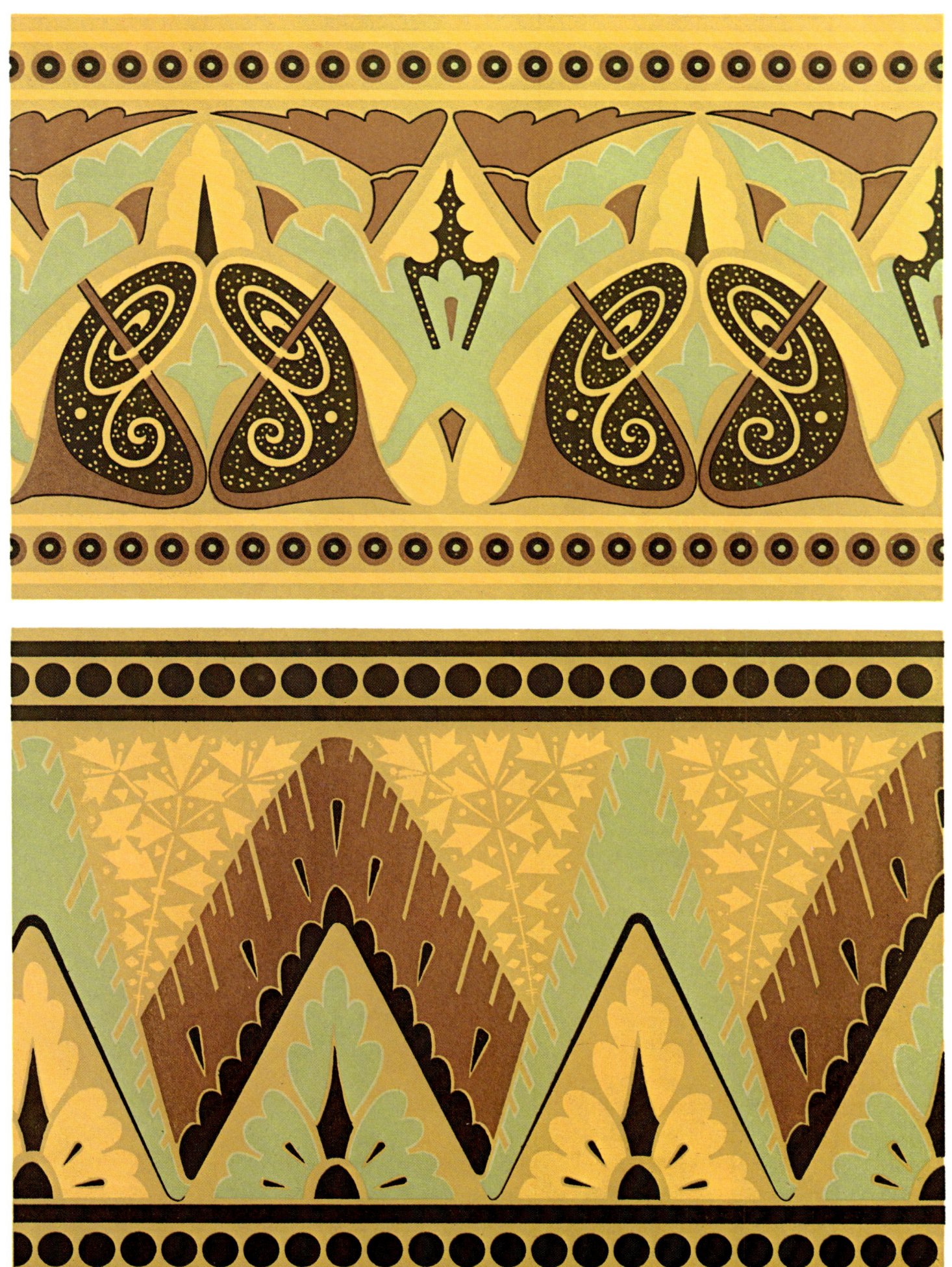

Two frieze ornaments or dado rails.

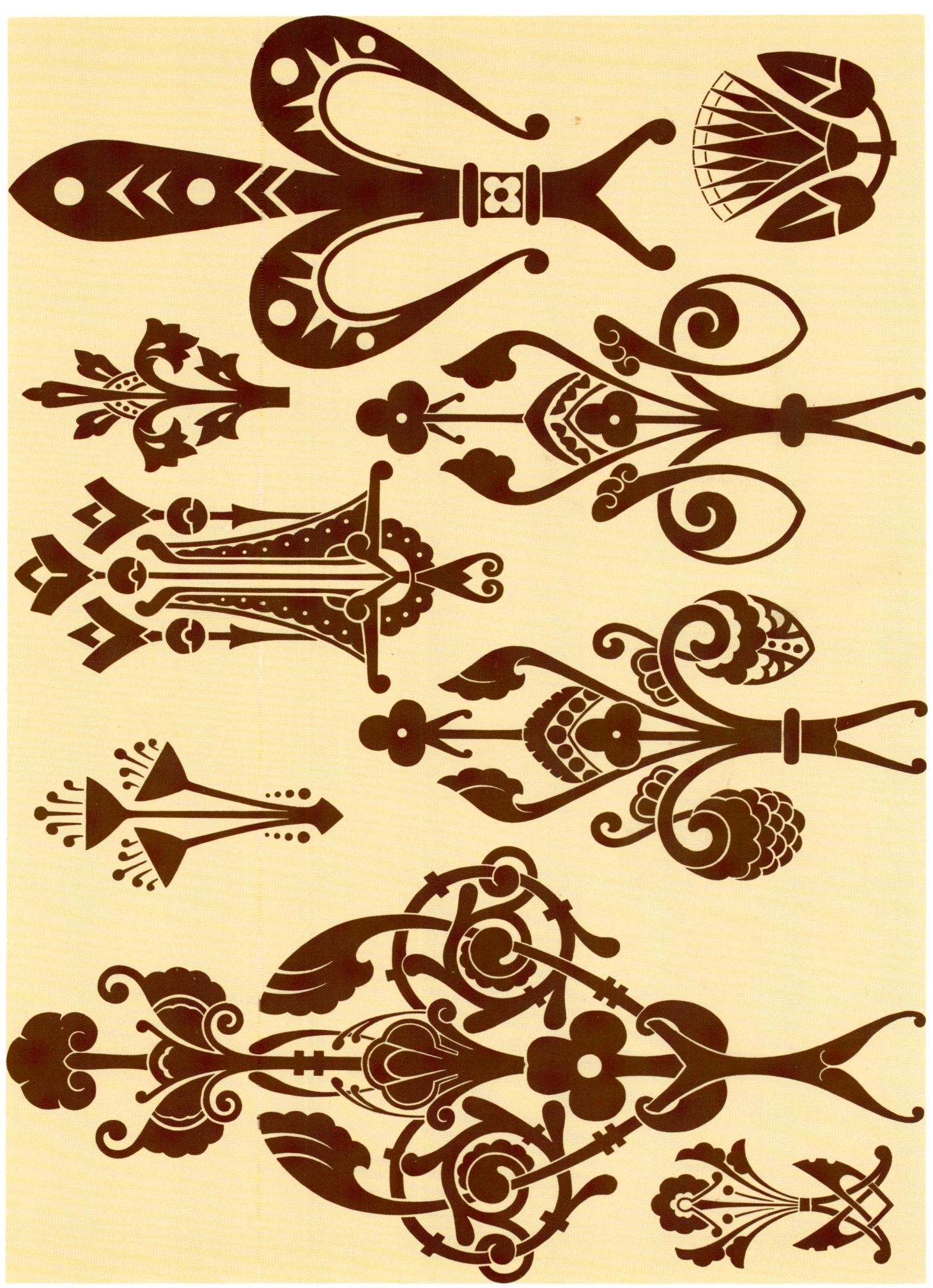

Powderings for stencilling on walls and dadoes.